# SHORT SENTENCE

## THREE YEARS IN DARTMOOR PRISON

*by*

Jessica Berens

This book is published by
Grosvenor House Publishing Ltd
28-30 High Street, Guildford, Surrey, GU1 3EL.
www.grosvenorhousepublishing.co.uk

A CIP record for this book
is available from the British Library

ISBN 978-1-78623-037-9

# INTRODUCTION

This is an account of the three years I spent as the Writer in Residence at Dartmoor prison in Devon. It is written as a series of episodic reflections with the intent of shedding light on some of the realities of prison life. Names have been changed to protect both the innocent and the guilty.

The Writers in Prison programme was organised by a small charity, the Writers in Prison Foundation, based in Wales. At its height there were over 20 Residencies established all over the prison estate meaning that prisoners of all ages and in all security categories were offered the chance to express themselves in informal and supportive settings that were flexible to both the regime and the needs of a nomadic and diverse population. Following the withdrawal of Arts Council funding these projects have now, by and large, disappeared.

Jessica Berens. Devon 2016

# ACKNOWLEDGEMENTS

With many thanks to the following for supplying both financial and moral support. The British Humane Association; John Fairbairn; the Writers in Prison Foundation; the Society of Authors; The Walter Guinness Charitable Trust; Fosbury; Yowlestone; Inside Time; Mr and Mrs Studholme; Duro Olowu; David Jenkins; Nick Davies; Kerri Sharp; Rachel Campbell-Johnston. Gang.

To Louise

# CONTENTS

# FOREWORD

By Nick Davies

Crime is complicated, and yet we deal with it as if it were all so simple.

A few years ago I spent some time researching a long series of stories for the Guardian about the criminal justice system and with dull regularity I ran into the same line being recycled by those who worked inside it: 'Criminal justice system? Well, we don't catch criminals and we don't dispense justice and it isn't a system but apart from that, yes, that's where I work.' Dull but they had a point.

At its core, we have a system which relies on two great simplicities - that we can detect the crimes which are committed and that we can deter criminals by punishing them. Those simplicities happen to have all the intellectual insight of a drunkard in a dark alley.

During that research for the *Guardian*, we crunched together the two best sources of statistics on the scale of crime and detection in the UK. The first is the British Crime Survey which annually questions more than 50,000 men, women and children about their experience as victims of crime. This has its limits but it's useful because it indicates the background picture of the amount of crime which is committed even if it is not reported to the police and/or not recorded by them. The second source is the collection of statistics filed for the Home Office by every police service in the country which indicates what happens once crimes are recorded: how many are investigated, detected and 'brought to justice'.

We merged both sets of statistics to get a crude snapshot of what happens to a typical 100 offences committed against people in the UK. How many offences are actually 'brought to justice', ie they end up with a guilty plea, a conviction or an offender asking for it to be 'taken into consideration' by a court. I reckoned the system was not that great, that we'd probably find that the success rate was only about 60%. I was wrong. Out of a typical 100 crimes, the real figure for the number brought to justice was... 3.

Having allowed 97% of crimes to escape all forms of criminal justice, the system then sets out to change the behaviour of those offenders who have been caught by punishing them.

That might make sense if you still believed some mediaeval fantasy that out there in the world there are good people and bad people and the bad people do bad things unless you threaten them with enough pain to deter them. At some point around the time when boys were being hanged for stealing chicken, it surely became clear that that theory needed a second look.

The same *Guardian* research threw up another interesting statistic, that 70% of the UK prison population suffered from at least two diagnosable personality disorders. There are a few serious bad guys in there - people who really are bad. But our courts and cells are clogged with thousands of hopeless, helpless men and women - neurotic, anxious, alcoholic, drug-addicted people who commit pathetic crimes for pathetic reasons. Threatening to hurt them doesn't figure in their landscape. Threatening to hurt them 3% of the time....

For sure, there are people who pick up the deterrent signal from the threat of punishment. They are law-abiding people. The 'system' can claim at least that much credit - that it reinforces the behaviour of people who were not inclined to misbehave. Beyond that, there is some kind of intellectual grand canyon between public opinion and reality.

It is completely understandable that public opinion wants to punish offenders. Anybody who is a victim of crime - or who imagines what it would be like to be one - feels angry, wants to hurt the bastard who hurt them. But human feelings are not necessarily a reliable guide to effective policy. What is more important? Getting angry or cutting crime?

I met police officers right up to the rank of chief constable who said they were fed up with arresting people; and magistrates and senior judges who said they were fed up with punishing people; and prison governors and prisons officers who perhaps more than any other group were really deeply fed up with what they were expected to do, 'warehousing' men and women. Most of these people were very clear about what they would like to be able to do.

The police were interested in 'problem solving' - reducing violence at football matches by putting seats into stadiums, stopping thefts in a rural car park by licensing an ice cream van, ending the war against drugs by providing a safe supply. They were interested too in pouring resources into intelligence-led policing so that instead of waiting for crimes to be committed and then hobbling around trying to detect them, they could identify the relatively small number of people in any community who tend to be prolific offenders and then deal with them.

The judges and the governors alike wanted to use social tools - education, employment, housing, psychotherapy. Somewhere in the mix, to be clear, they expected punishment to play some part. But not to be the whole damn system. But they have no chance of getting their way. Too much anger in the way, too much tabloid stupidity. So we carry on sentencing, carry on warehousing, carry on building more and more prisons.

Nick Davies was an investigative reporter for the *Guardian* for thirty-seven years. He is the author of the best-selling book *Hack Attack: How the truth caught up with Rupert Murdoch*.

# 1. MURDER

The road to Dartmoor prison, an antediluvian commute, runs through a prehistoric landscape dotted with enigmatic granite growths and the sodden green of blanket bog. The moor is a bizarre wilderness quickly cut off by snow and fog and rain; the winds actually whistle and the white mists really do swirl, as if to purposely please the tourists that arrive with expectations of gothic legend.

Conan Doyle described a valley of fear in Devonshire, haunted by the *Hound of the Baskervilles*, all desolate and sinister and full of mud that swallowed ponies. The moor does have moments of melancholy but, when the sun is on it, it is resplendent and mysterious, thanks to millions of years of climatic event and the intrusion of granite through various lavas.

The granite is still exposed, taking different shapes depending on what has happened to it and when. Some of the strange grey growths on the landscape are where Neolithic people built their chambered tombs. Bronze age men made inexplicable stone circles and, later, when God appeared, so too did the indestructible Medieval stone crosses hammered immutably into the grass verges, pointing the way to various abbeys.

The weather is so persistently cold and wet it has affected local house prices, which remain as stagnant as the damp on their bedroom walls. It gets everywhere, the damp, creeping and smelling and staining. It's not easy, this bit of Devon so, unsurprisingly, Real Life keeps a low profile – its symbols are few.

The Dartmoor ponies, cartoon shaped with short legs and barrel stomachs, stand in line beside the ice cream van as if they are queuing to buy a cone; sheep can occasionally be spotted, bright pink, as the dye of their branding runs in the rain. Both species wander about gormlessly in the middle of the road, occasionally ambling in front of cars, oblivious to their death wish.

Princetown, named in 1809 for the future George IV (fat 'Bertie'), is the name of the nearest village to HMP Dartmoor and was built to serve the prison. It is reached by a narrow moor road, once the route of packhorses, and is easily cut off by snow which means that the drug workers can't get their cars through, while the prison officers who live in Princetown walk to work, crunching up the hill in their big black HMP-issue boots.

Even if a civilian (teachers, nurses and so on) can push the hatchback through in the morning, snowfall in the day can prevent exit, particularly from the visitors' car park, where the hill out to the road can become covered with ice and turn into a Death Slope.

Some swear that in the past snowfall was so high that officers had to dig their way into work. One long-serving man claimed he had once walked across the snowy moor chained to a team of colleagues. Nowadays special buses pick employees up from outside Morrisons and everyone makes their way in gingerly, slipping on the ice, regularly falling over and breaking various limbs so there are huddled conversations about litigation.

The actual stone portal to Dartmoor is the famous arch of its legend and the photograph of its heritage brand. It arrived when the prison was built, in various stages, during the early nineteenth century, and bears the Latin motif *Parcere Subjectis* – Spare the Vanquished – which meant little then and even less now since the prison has never spared anyone, its history being one of brutality, dehumanisation and violence both for the prisoners and the men who contained them.

The outer gateway is not actually the entrance in to the prison. A door into the gate lodge is the entrance, once manned by grinning men in white shirts who welcomed you in and manually handed over your keys. Now, thanks to expensive modernisation, it is a computerised set of locked cupboards, which are opened with a biometric fingerprint. The grinning men retired to a domain behind a locked door where they peered at the images from the CCTV cameras and could only be contacted by radio or telephone, and sometimes not even then if there was only one person on duty doing everything.

It was a typical Friday morning in November 2015. Rain came down on the head, and cold damp seeped into the chest. There was an (incorrect) rumour that TB had arrived on the wings. 'Intelligence', as it was known, had identified the presence of heroin on G Wing. A Mr D was insisting that he was being contacted by a government agency and that he intended to become a serial killer. L had smashed his television and was threatening to kill a sex offender. F was smoking legal highs and writing on the walls of his cell. It was, in other words, business as usual.

I was Quebec 38.

'Quebec 38 to M2OD, Jessica Berens, permission to join the net, over . . .'

'Quebec 38, good signal . . .'

The rest of the shift signed on over their radios – the Oscars and Papas, tired voices of uniforms starting their shifts; posh voices of middle-class librarians; jokey voices from the workshop instructors who knew the community well; an unexpected South African accent, and the less experienced who said, 'Thank you very much,' and 'Goodbye,' and 'How do you switch this thing on?' rather than 'Over and out.'

I wasn't scared of the radio any more, though it had taken some time to adjust to it, not only to affix it correctly on to the side of the body so it didn't poke out like a lever, but to ensure I didn't press the red emergency button by mistake, meaning that every officer in the vicinity would come running (at the various paces dictated by age and comportment) across the icy grey yards in order to save my life.

There was also an emergency button in every room, green, and usually near the light switch, so that also got pressed by mistake, particularly by newcomers, but sometimes for a laugh by troublemakers on G Wing, so that notices had to go up saying, This Is Not A Light Switch.

MO was the first to arrive at about 8 a.m.

'I'm surprised you're in, Jess.'

'Why's that then?'

'There was a murder yesterday afternoon.'

'You're joking.'

I thought he was joking, actually, as he quite often joked. He once bought in a 'show and tell' item he had found in the food, holding up a slimy, grey, rubbery tube about three inches long. Half an hour of guessing what it was (and, worse, where it came from) produced several gag responses but no firm conclusion. The gloomy matter had a pronounced valve and looked like the section of an animal's alimentary canal. It haunted me for days. The Thing.

MO was fifty-eight and in for an historic sex offence.

'No, yeah. Someone got stabbed in the kitchen.'

Officer or prisoner was my next question.

'Prisoner . . . small fella . . . Polish lad. I didn't know him.'

Time started to move very slowly, as it always does in the warp of sudden violence. I walked calmly to the man who ran the workshop nearest to my classroom. We worked at the opposite ends of a peculiar suite where prefabricated classrooms had been constructed alongside each other like a railway carriage, in order to preserve the exterior stone walls, which were granite and listed.

'Did you know there had been a murder?'

'Yeah, sort of.'

'Has there ever been one when you have been working here?'

No. He had been in his workshop for twenty years.

The prisoners started to file up the metal staircase, some turning left to go to Contracts 2 (desktop publishing) some turning right to come to Creative Writing, a three-hour session that I ran and which, over the three years I had worked as the Writer in Residence, had entertained an array of characters and a variety of projects arguably connected with self-expression.

I had arrived in Dartmoor in 2012. My remit was to support arts activities, a loose brief, and it needed to be. Prescription has little place in a C Cat regime and even less in the arcane and personal processes that are writing and art. I started by running Creative Writing and Magazine Production sessions, then organised some hobby and music groups because there was a demand for them.

Projects ranged from poetry and cartoons to screenplays and calligraphy. We had made villages out of matches, books out of wallpaper and written a radio play where Sweep was recast as a werewolf. I had been purposely flexible because, as today was to prove, everything can change in a second.

I don't quite know how I had ended up with ten computers and a room of my own; certainly I had not specifically asked for it. Procurement of resources remained a complete mystery to me. I simply didn't know how anybody got anything and a Requisition Order did not make things any clearer, bearing, as it did, the secret code of prison language that asked for budget holder signatures and other authorisations.

However, I had observed the ebb and flow of assets and marvelled as they manifested miraculously around the prison. New carpets often appeared overnight, for no obvious reason, as did piles of tables and chairs and boxes full of abandoned lever arch files.

I had also observed and admired the officers who carved empires into the many deserted enclaves of the prison. One, who was working in a basement full of corridors and abandoned cells, told me she had, 'put in a business strategy'. The result was a department, sometimes called 'Diversity', where wheelchairs were repaired and mushrooms were grown. Very old men would repair from their wings. Some of them painted pictures of Easter rabbits on to wooden spoons or made strange musical instruments with only one hole and one note. M, who had had a stroke, listened to 'The Great Rock and Roll Swindle' while crouched over a table on which there was a jigsaw puzzle. Unable to speak, he would wave the CD cover with his one good hand to show you what it was.

Some of the old men had had full professional lives and took over the administration duties. They wrote the rotas for cleaning, for instance, or the distribution list for the newspapers. Some of them spent the morning counting and packing sachets of sugar. While many of them enjoyed bickering with each other, others could not engage. They sat on the comfortable chairs, stared into space, and waited for death.

Another member of staff, a teacher, had led teams of prisoners bearing tables and chairs into an abandoned cell on F Wing and made it into a classroom.

At the beginning of the Residency I didn't have an office and carried the various folders and lunch items around in a shopping bag on wheels. An officer suggested I move into the recently abandoned Shannon Trust office on G5. This looked tempting as it was newly painted, white and red, and had a computer and a telephone. But it was on G5, the frontline, the fifth landing, high up on G Wing. Arguably the most dangerous place in the prison, it was known, locally, as 'Beirut'.

Men were in for drugs, violence, aggravated burglary, incidents involving weapons, beating up the missus, beating up a random stranger, murder. Younger, careless, disenfranchised, disassociated, bored, volatile, they were immersed in a culture of 'nonce hatred', drug-taking, fighting, bullying and the various troubles that beset a prison, such as phone smuggling, drug smuggling and distilling illicit alcohol or 'hooch'.

If the general alarm went it was usually because there was trouble on G Wing. The day the security department closed down the whole prison and implemented a surprise search they found ten home-made knives there. It's a very nasty thing, the chiv. Made of plastic and found metal, its only purpose is to cause serious harm. This meant that one had to look at everything through the eyes of a scared maniac and worry about what everything could be fashioned into. Practically anything can be made into a weapon by a frightened person with too much time on his hands and rising levels of debt. I lost a spiral-bound notebook once and didn't sleep for three nights, imagining the wire as a garrotte.

G Wing also happened to be one of the largest and the highest of the wings. It was crowded and a lot of men in track-suits were always milling around, shaven headed, spotted, watching television in each other's cells, complaining, non-compliant, and unemployed. Everyone looked as if they were up to something, even if they weren't. If they had transferred from a Young Offender Institution, Feltham say, or Portland, they knew only prison-made friends, fighting, drugs and the streets. They were leering, lairy, defended, insouciant. And quite often high.

'G Wing' were the ones most likely to resort to going on the roof, known as Incident at Height. They might, for instance, clamber on top of the Portakabin in front of the chapel. Then 600 prisoners would be banged up while the duties of the prison officers were re-routed to deal with the roof situation, on one occasion undermined by a local Devon newspaper which claimed that the protesters had been offered sun-cream.

The end game tended to see the protesters come down for tea, go on record, transfer to Seg (the Segregation Unit, or ' block') and likely out of the prison. Their names would go onto the file known as 'Active Alerts' with a one-word warning – 'Climber'.

Incidents at Height were greeted with fury by the rest of the prisoner population, who suffered the consequent bang up, and boredom by the prison officers who had seen it all before and had to ensure that the dissidents didn't hurt themselves or anyone else.

The reasons for a protest on the roof (once established by a trained negotiator and some shouting) were usually the same as the reasons for protests on the wing: the agitators wanted to move prisons to be nearer family or further away from debt.

The debtors, and debt, incited an estimated 30 per cent of violent and disruptive incidents. Individuals acted out, moved to Seg and out of the prison. Borrowing and running away was a familiar syndrome recognised by the regime and criticised by other prisoners who, despite the confusing lights shed by the moral prism, saw debtors as thieves.

Fortunately or unfortunately, depending on your opinions about public spending, the youths on G Wing had no idea how to commit a crime without getting caught.

The cells on G Wing were all close together, so it really mattered if the man next door was noisy – loud thumping bass in particular made everyone go mad. This enduring problem in prison life was ever present and sometimes complex, since the prisoners with mental health problems were often the ones who needed to escape the hell of their inner life by immersing their beings into bass; take the noise away and you have inner noise, acting out, cutting, and other problems that staff knew they were ill-equipped to address.

A prisoner on G Wing was described as 'G Wing' – as it became a shorthand description of an individual. 'Is he G Wing?' meant, 'Is he an uneducated, miserable, volatile delinquent whose current behavioural issues are more than likely to be drug related?'

Other prisoners were described as being on a wing rather than being the wing itself. 'Is he on B wing?' meant that he was probably a sex offender, but his wing did not define him. Strangely prison argot allowed the sex offender to step beyond definition and towards change, while a 'main' prisoner was seen as forever G Wing, unchanging and unchangeable, unfairly for those G Wing individuals who were trying to achieve qualifications and/or abstinence.

A senior governor vetoed the idea of my moving into the abandoned office on G5, so I moved books and papers, files and bargain Biros into a former cell in the new Induction Suite.

The new Induction Suite was a scarlet sea of lovely wall-to-wall carpeting and the old heavy metal cell doors had been tricked out with bright-blue glossy paint. The furniture was new. You knew the notice boards were new because their glass was still intact and the locks were still on them and they were inhabited by fairly current information about Equality and Safeguarding.

On a desk there were neat arrangements of information for the newcomer on the panorama of their possibilities in the realm of jobs and education. A Diploma in Bricklaying, for instance, could lead to an NVQ Level 2 in Trowel Occupations. You could go for a BICS Level 1 in 'practical cleaning skills' or an NOCN Level 1 Progression Award in Family Relationships and Developing Parenting Skills.

Job 'opportunities' included Light Textiles (making green trousers for prisoners) Laundry and Waste Management.

All was clean in the Induction Suite, if incredibly warm, so warm in fact that I did occasionally fall asleep in it – but around the corner, a locked gate away, there was a crepuscular corridor where the lights had a horror movie flicker. One wall was lined with doors studded and padlocked by heavy rusting chains. A grimy fissure allowed a peeper's eye to squint into a crumbling cell full of some past purpose – 'HR' the sign said in Biro on a bit of cardboard, and there were rotting records in folders on unbalanced rusting shelves lit by a small barred rectangle that was a basement window looking out onto a grey stone wall.

Years ago this row of cells was said to have contained men who were judged to be insane – insanity, of course, being very much defined by the contemporaneous regulator rather than any realistic clinical definition of which I am aware.

The atmosphere of this corridor was profuse with misery – you knew it before you were told it. And I was not the only one to think so. Several women said they did not want to be there alone. One did not expect paranormal occurrence as such, but there was an old stagnant energy of despondency, shackled and trapped, that one did not feel on either side of this corridor.

Then a room in what used to be an Education Suite became available. It had ten computers that, in terms of prison resources, was NASA. The Education Department didn't want it, their own rooms were nicer and newer and they liked to stick together in a green prefabricated building next to B Wing where they could put up their laminated notices about Level One Maths and where, when I first arrived, a large rat lived in the loo.

A senior officer of wit and experience suggested I put a plaque with my name on it, like a flag on a mountain, and then the room would be mine. I did and it worked! I got a huge brick-like plaque made in Carps bearing the message 'Jessica Berens, Writer in Residence', and I made an office in the tiny glass receptacle that was a server room. It was an easy conquest because, unlike Kuwait, nobody wanted it.

Little by little the room had become my centre of operations personalised by the product of achievement and ennobled with the puerile aesthetic of a school common room where there was a sign saying 'No Singing' and Colin's ridiculous rendition of Dildo Man, a superhero disfigured with felt-penned phalli that made him laugh for ages.

The underground spirit was given an authentic atmosphere by the fact that the Suite with No Name bore some resemblance to a car boot sale where the cars had been bought and the owners had left the stuff behind. Its acoustics, notoriously awful, were one of the reasons why the rooms had been spurned by the Education Department. It was like sitting on the runway at Heathrow; one had to shout over the constant whir of a huge heating fan and listen to every voice in every other classroom. Added to this, birds on the roof, the carpentry workshop underneath and the occasional ukulele workshop meant there was far too much shouting, which is never wise in a secure setting where shouting can mean so many different things. I was constantly yelling, 'What!?' as if I needed an ear trumpet. And then I had to lean close to the men to hear them, body contact had to be avoided, so I was always unnaturally contorted.

There was an abandoned karaoke machine and a euphonium that nobody could resist the temptation to pretend to blow whilst making noises as if they were playing it. There were piles of dusty old lever arch files containing wrinkled archives pertaining to enigmatic pursuits such as CLAIT and forgotten folders whose insides revealed long- abandoned educational aspirations in the form of Skills for Life Entry Level 3. It was post-apocalyptic and there was more dust than in *The Road*.

The facilities for staff refreshment were contained in a small glass cubicle where there was a fridge, an electric kettle and some china mugs. Some departments had microwaves but there was no 'mess' for the officers on long shifts who had travelled through the dark and snow to get to work; no mess and no beds in the event that they were forced to remain in the prison because of the weather.

There was a wooden cupboard in the 'kitchenette' that held the keys to other cupboards whose identity and locks were a mystery until they were explained by one long-term prisoner who knew exactly which cupboard held what contents and which key went into each lock. This could have been seen as suspicious (the press had described this individual as a 'Jekyll and Hyde' character) but many misgivings are put aside in a quest for a hole-puncher. A hole-puncher doesn't sound like much until you haven't got one – like everything really.

Teachers labelled their stuff with Tippex and were possessive over the ownership of anything from paper to staplers to sharpeners.

'If you don't bring it back I'll kill you,' became my intemperate instruction to the prisoners who borrowed a sharpener.

One wall bore a collage that Colin had made from articles and pictures torn from *Tor Views*, the prison magazine; another was taken up by the magazine covers produced over ten years through innumerable production methods, colour photocopying and so on, and displaying the eternal issues of prison life – from the work of the Offender Management Unit to How to Complain to what to do about birds getting in the way of the television aerials and ruining the TV reception on D Wing.

There was also a wooden cow, a Triffid-like houseplant that had responded well to prison conditions, and the Koestler arts certificates which bore testaments to prizes won in the annual prison arts awards.

A graphic designer had made jokey cartoons of kitchen workers and a filing cabinet was full of glue and glitter and saved cardboard. Laminated pictures bore countryside images and poetry written by a young man, in for violence, who wanted to apologise to his mum.

I hung onto the optimistic notion that something could be made in this absurd universe, an optimism encouraged by the practical reality that, in amongst all the dirt and debris, the computers actually worked. It meant that something could be designed and written, albeit on ancient and outdated software.

There was, however, no internet, no scanner and no printer on account of the fact that a member of staff had removed the one that did work and replaced it with an identical one that did not work because it had not been connected to the relevant computers. The member of staff who had the secret knowledge had then gone to hospital taking (allegedly) an Important Red File and some key passwords so nobody knew what the hell was going on with the computers. Well, I certainly didn't. The prisoners did. That was what many of them were in for, after all – downloading.

The only problem with occupying this territory was, like many newly colonised lands, nobody knew what to call it, which meant that nobody knew where it was, which meant that it was difficult to tell either duty officers or prisoners where it was: 'You know, above plastering, next to textiles, up the metal stairs, opposite the Multi-Faith Room, no, yes, not Thinking Skills, they've moved, haven't they, into that hut by G Wing? No that's A Wing – SMS? Not there, no that doesn't exist anymore, which direction are you coming from . . . ?' And so on.

The prison's inseparable domains were linked by murky passageways where interminable rusty gates creaked and squeaked and led not to the planned destination but into freezing yards (spotted with orange peel) and razor-wired pens and the decrepit hinterlands of the prison's long history. Go past the library, through the line of grey tracksuits queuing to receive medical care, through four locks, several barred gates and into a blast of freezing moor wind, past a discarded ping pong ball (could be full of drugs, might not be), and bits of loo roll and prisoners emerging from the 'CARAT' (drug team) office. A lot of them have their hands down their trousers jiggling their unused appendages.

'If you want to stay sane,' one prisoner advised, 'learn quickly that time moves at a different pace inside these walls. Even the things you think are really, really important will seem to take forever to sort out. Prison is an institution and a bureaucracy so don't be surprised if five different people tell you five different ways to do the same thing.'

Lost on many occasions, I had concluded that the prison's indecipherable signage and pointless passageways symbolised the wider truth of the penal system, where long-term maladministration and short-term policy thinking have woven a web from which it is almost impossible for an individual to disentangle himself. There was little logic and, where it did exist, or sensible intention lurked, progress had been fatally obstructed for decades by the apparently insurmountable schism between enlightened vision and an operational reality where there were few frontline staff, demoralised department heads, and no money.

So, like hundreds of Josef Ks, men with no lives, no prospects and no teeth leaned endlessly over the balconies and stared down through the safety net, swallowed up, subsumed and lost. Many had to stay where they were purely because they could not complete the courses that had been prescribed to change their 'offending behaviour' because the courses did not exist in the prison to which they had been transferred.

Signs and arrows pointed to departments and wings but, like most signs and arrows in my experience, they do not often synchronise with the reality of the environment they are supposed to be signifying.

Blue notice boards around the corridors cited the alarming semiotics of prison life. 'Crying Alone?' 'Suicide and Self Harm Policy Statement', 'Stop the Violence', 'Need help? Call the Samaritans?' 'NOMS Equality Statement (fairness for all)' and that sinister yellow square that informs you of 'Danger by Death' and has a silhouette of a little man being stabbed by a bolt of lightning.

Though now, a little man had been stabbed by a knife in the kitchen.

## 2. WHAT'S FOR TEA?

By 8.10 a.m. Dan had arrived with most of the news as, for some reason, everyone always told him everything, probably because he asked incessant personal questions that were difficult to deflect. 'Why don't you drink, Jess?' for example, though not as bad as Colin, who persistently asked if I was a lesbian.

Me: 'I'm not a lesbian, Colin, as far as I know.'

Colin: 'So why can't we get married then?'

Me: 'For reasons far too numerous to list.'

Dan was clever and relatively sane. He was what a journalist would call a reliable source, despite the fact that he was serving a sentence for cocaine distribution. He had achieved some local notoriety and a case where the prosecution had described kitchens and underground networks communicating by text messages in code.

He was not, however, Pablo Escobar. He had operated from his bedroom in his parents' house and had made an apparent profit of £18,000, for which he got seven years and had to hand over his flash car, which he insisted had been acquired from the legitimate profits made from organising raves. One got the impression that there had been quite a lot of personal use and the fun had got out of control. Dan said he would never take drugs again and he was enjoying rehabilitative sessions with the popular women of the Substance Misuse Team, whom he described as 'fit' and who had a huge suite of rooms on A wing. He (like everyone else) was upset when one of the Substance Misuse counsellors was 'walked out' of the prison following an incident whose truth remained hidden but, depending on who you asked, involved anything from alcohol to condoms. Anyway, everyone said she had been walked out in tears and it was a shame.

Dan, aged twenty-five, very easily bored, had embarked on an enormous novel of fantastic complexity to which he dedicated his time with enthusiasm and which made me think of him as both original and publishable.

He and his mates, other clever middle-class reprobates, huddled in corners trying to work out their POCA and imitating my public school accent when I pronounced it POKER. They were right, the O was o as in the 'of' in Proceeds of Crime Act. Fraudsters, dealers (and their lawyers) had to work out how much they owed the government from the profits they had supposedly made from selling dope, a complex equation informed by the chimerical value of street units.

By 8.30 Dan had spoken to a Listener who knew the victim. The Listeners are trained by the Samaritans, trained to listen to the dawn anxieties of men who are often terrified, occasionally remorseful. The Listeners talk to the suicidal and this one knew the little fella, so details began to filter through.

A big Scouser had taken offence with a younger Pole while they had both been chopping vegetables. There had been a brief verbal exchange and the big Scouser had shoved the knife he was holding into the Polish man. Apparently it had been all about potatoes. That was what K said, anyway.

They had all been taken back to their cells in the middle of the afternoon of the previous day. They had seen the arrival of the air ambulance through the chinks in the windows of their cells and some said that they had heard the victim dying over the radio as officers ran up and down the corridor communicating the emergency to each other. It was a code blue, then red – apparently Healthcare didn't have the training for a stabbing. The victim bled out on the floor of the kitchen.

People were saying they had seen the Oscar One (duty manager) with blood all over her.

There was no question of doing much work. Everyone had to process this and cope.

'What happened about tea?' I asked.

Food was a constant source of morbid fascination to the 600 or so men who had to eat it and was a mainstay of conversation, as was the perceived filth, dishonesty and incompetence of the 'kitchen'.

The industrial kitchen was the domain of the Catering Manager, a middle-aged man condemned to wear a nylon trilby. His department was made of stainless steel cauldrons and piles of bulk-bought sliced white bread. Around him were sacks of potatoes and cabbages and vast tins of baked beans. There were also fifty or so men recruited from the landings, involved in various NVQ food safety and handling qualifications and regularly caught red-handed stealing supplies. One kitchen worker raided a fridge by unscrewing a panel at the back, extricating rashers of bacon and winding them around his thighs underneath his trousers. They (rashers not thighs) would have attracted a good price on the wing, though how they were going to be cooked in a kettle ignited some speculation.

The prisoners who worked in the kitchen were sometimes accused of fishing the meat out of the dishes and eating it before it was wheeled on to the wings, meaning that curries were soup by the time they reached the queue of diners. Meat was rarely provided in significant quantities and men talked about it with misty-eyed sentiment. Ask a prisoner who is about to leave the prison what his first meal will be and he will inevitably say a, 'steak' or a 'Big Mac', depending on the characteristics of his background. Some want to go to the pub, the younger ones miss drugs, but most are starved of protein and long for meat.

The Catering Manager's job was to feed 600 men on a budget of around £1.87 per person per day. This minute sum, the tax payer may or may not be pleased to know, tends to be cut year on year, meaning that the food becomes ever whiter and portions smaller, as the health of the ageing population of the prison system becomes more chronic and expensive.

The food had to be bought from official government 'suppliers', meaning the prison could not source local produce from the Devon farming community or, for that matter, work the farm that existed on its own land. It was the government's suppliers who tended to be at the centre of any food scandal that arises; around cheap meat contaminated with horse and so on. More than one joke was made about how the population of Dartmoor ponies was dwindling as local newspapers described suspect findings in the meat supplied to the prison.

The minutiae of provision were detailed in depth by instructions from the National Offender Management Service, whose emissions were as numerous as the crowds of civil servants stationed at NOMS HQ in Petty France.

The Catering Manager had to comply with directions supplied by The NOMS Head of Catering & Physical Education Services who, with Directors of Offender Management, monitored, 'mandatory outputs'.

The Catering Manager's job was to, 'provide meals for prisoners which were planned, procured, prepared and served in the, 'correct manner', taking into account 'provider procurement rules', 'health and safety legislation', 'food hygiene legislation' and 'national security framework' guidelines.

The Catering Manager's menu was closely monitored and scrutinised so that 'commissioners' could, 'measure/obtain assurance on the delivery of the outputs/output features'. But, 'where an output/output feature does not have Performance Indicator(s) or Management Information associated with it, then it is proposed that it should be covered by Assurance Statements and Contract/SLA Management and/or audit of the service by NOMS Audit and Corporate Assurance (ACA).'

The Catering Manager's skill set doubtless included the admirable ability to understand what this meant, as he successfully transmogrified Prison Service Instruction into a cold lunch handed out at around 12 noon after prisoners filed back to the wings after work and education. Lunch tended to be sandwiches, baguettes, the odd (in every sense of the word) salad, soup and piece of fruit.

The day's hot meal, tea, was served at around five. There would be, on various evenings, curries, casseroles, pies and pasta dishes, chicken legs, fish and snack packs, with the additional choice of rice or potatoes, another vegetable (carrots, cabbage or peas), with a further choice of sweet or fruit (rice pudding, sponge and custard, apple or orange).

Tea, served on plastic and eaten with plastic, was a singularly joyless experience, bereft of any commune, disturbed by fights triggered by the perception of unfair portions, disturbed by the paedophiles talking dirty behind you, accompanied by the revolting smell that is institution cooking and full of the perils of foreign objects which were then described in detail to whoever would listen.

One-downmanship began with, 'Pubic hair and worse . . .' and continued to, '. . . why is the fish pie orange?'

Meals were picked by prisoners from a menu sheet on which tiny pigs and chickens supposedly denoted for whose diet the meal was appropriate but, in true Prison Service style, there was no guide as to what the symbols meant. A Turkish flag floated randomly alongside 'cheese flan'; there was a cow next to the 'jumbo sausage baguette'; a heart next to 'coronation chicken pasta' and V for the bean and potato curry. Floating cabbages provided mysterious significance to fruited semolina and vegetarian Bolognese.

Prisoners received this list once a week, on Fridays, chose from five lunch-time and five tea-time options each day for the two weeks ahead, then handed it in to the landing office on Sunday.

Meals were prepared throughout the morning and afternoon, placed in chafer dishes and kept in cold or hot boxes until collected by wing workers prior to serving. There was a small servery on the ground floor of each wing containing a server counter, into which food was placed.

Prisoners were called landing by landing, where they queued for their food, which the senior orderly then called from the list chosen previously. Servery workers dished out the chosen food onto the plastic plates and bowls that prisoners kept in their cells. Bread and butter was collected from a hatch and men returned to their cells to eat the meal with plastic cutlery while sitting next to their loos. Food waste was either placed in the small cell bin or washed down the toilet, and everything was then washed in the cell sink, also next to the loo.

Each wing had one 'chip nite', talked about as something to look forward to, unlike the boiled potatoes whose consistency stimulated comments that vegetables were not washed before being cooked.

The Catering Manager's response to this was to advise prisoners that the potatoes were not peeled but scrubbed by hand, in order to conserve the health-giving properties of the potato skin.

The breakfast pack was given to everyone at teatime for the following morning. This contained a small bag of cereal, a small carton of UHT milk, four tea bags, four sugars and four whiteners. The prison-issued tea bags were considered to be a waste of time and piles of them were regularly found in the rubbish by the recycling workers who couldn't trade them for love or money, not that either featured in life on the wings, tobacco being the currency: tobacco, drugs, bananas, art work. And sex, if you believed everything you heard.

Prisoners were given 2–4 slices of bread and 1–2 pats of butter at teatime, and each night an additional portion of either biscuits, crisps or kitchen-made cakes. One piece of toast was provided with weekend lunch and that was also seen as a treat, something to talk about and regard with excitement.

I assumed, naively, that Christmas would provide brief respite from the white diet. Being somewhat neurotic about the profound misery of Christmas myself, I incorrectly projected this element of my own reality on to a population where, in fact, this festival was almost completely irrelevant beyond the tinselled reminder of families lost and lives misspent.

Colin, who had been in prison for most of his 24-year-long life, remembered one winter at Aylesbury Prison, an institution where the young offenders were lifers, which meant they had committed very serious crimes before the age of 21. Christmas, he said, was cancelled due to the fact that the majority of the population were Muslim. The Muslims then staged a riot, broke into a workshop, and armed themselves with hammers and chisels. 'All we could see from the wing were the riot squads marching up to the mosque all kitted up, flash grenades the lot. It was all over the news . . . it was my claim to fame for a while.'

A Dartmoor lifer, in for violence, had started his sentence in HMP Liverpool in 2005. He wrote about a festive period where the loneliness was more pronounced than usual and where the snow blew onto his face due to the fact that he was on the upper bunk and exposed to a permanently broken window. It was cold, and wearing every garment available to him did not help much. A school dinner turkey was provided by disinterested officers and the film was *The Railway Children*. Grendon was better – an enlightened therapeutic community that changed his life, and the dinners were eaten together. In Dartmoor he and his mates ate their Christmas dinner whilst sitting on settees on the wings and he thought about the possibilities of life outside and a daughter he had not seen grow up. 'She was nine years old when I was sentenced. Now she is nineteen, at university, and I don't know her.'

MO, who had been in hospitality, was very interested in food and wrote about it as part of his creative writing pursuits. Cooking in the cell kettle was officially prohibited but MO managed to combine items bought from the canteen (the list of groceries they were allowed to buy on a weekly basis with their private money) with food provided by the prison to create 'in-cell cuisine'.

'Keep the mashed potato that is served with tea,' he suggested. 'Mix it with couscous bought from canteen. Add cheese from the evening snack pack. HEY PRESTO! Close your eyes; it's scrambled egg!'

He was an excellent writer. One article he contributed to the prison magazine was particularly vivid.

**FEEDING TIME**

'FOURS,' bellows out an ex-Army Sergeant Major-type officer, from three landings below (about sixty feet).

His shouting resonates through the building, and kick-starts a stampede of hungry shaven- headed Wildebeest, who now storm their way down to the food servery from their landing. He looks like a demented vulture, black body, big

26

white chest, strained pink neck, as he shouts out again, spittle flying through the air. He has triggered their twice-daily expedition to ground floor level, to collect their pre-ordered food.

They clatter along the steel landings, weaving, squeezing, shoving, corralled between grey-painted brick walls and painted steel doors to one side, with steel grid handrails and fencing to the other side. The herd clusters into a passageway of about 1.2 metres wide. The fencing prevents them from falling or diving into a huge atrium that goes from the grey vinyl floor below, up to a pitched galvanised roof, groaning under the strain of keeping a lid on the fear, noise and smells of the multitude.

Light pierces through the roof lights and shimmers via the frosted glazed gable end windows, bouncing off the paintwork, flickering with shadows. The seething mass moves at different speeds from shuffle to gallop, down the caged tunnel, finally appearing from nowhere, amidst the Dartmoor Serengeti, to their evening watering hole.

They arrive at the bottom landing, ground floor, a clearing enclosed by the same disheartening mixture of grey walls and doors, incorporating two pool tables, a table tennis table, and two fish tanks along one side. Forming a queue, snorting and stomping impatiently, they are herded into an orderly channel by more irate vultures.

By now they are panting, eyes full of anticipation, peering right, left, up, down, and across the small clearing, in case of attack.

They are wearing either their prison clothes (blue jeans, blue T-shirts, black pumps) or a mixture of all sorts and brands of casual gear of their choice, dependant on fashion status, and what they were allowed to bring in with them. Trainers are the biggest icon, enhancing their hooves, the cost, establishing their position in prison hierarchy.

A cold shiver ripples down their necks to their backs, as they are herded through a single door entrance to the food servery itself, to face a pack of white-hatted hyenas glaring from behind a glazed stainless steel counter.

Six pairs of eyes immediately transfix on them, staring and scowling, as they enter their lair. The group instantly transforms into a line of nervous jittering fatal forms.

Faced by the demonic leader of the pack, each member of the herd stutters out its cell number, whereby the boss immediately growls back with 'Three, potato, sweet.' This gives them their main, veg and dessert (fruit or pud) option. The creatures sidle along, confronted by slathering brutes that dump their food onto blue plastic plates by spoon or hand, grunting only. This whole exercise lasts nothing more than 20 seconds per animal, when they spring back out through another door opening, back onto the main atrium.

They exhale a huge sigh of relief through their mouths and nostrils, closing their eyes, then, re-focusing on a small hatch, to the side, they go and pick up 4 slices of bread, (white or brown) and two pats of butter.

They are now at the bottom of the opposite sets of metal checker plate stairs, used for ascending only, at meal times, back to their landing. Down at this level, the sun provides for a hazy light diffusing down from the roof, melting through the railings and nettings.

A further number of hyenas are hanging over the edges baying like the Romans in the Coliseum. As the mass starts its climb, the scavengers glower and spit at them, waiting for the weak ones to stumble and fall, 'Give us your bread, give us your rock cake, give us your jelly' and so on.

The mob pushes its way through, and up, to its own landing, and returns to its respective homes, doors being kicked closed creating a loud simultaneous and tumultuous echo, as metal planks slam into metal frames.

They are safe to eat their meals, in peace, once more.

**Prisoners thought and talked about their health a lot, as they deteriorated into a 'Dad's Army' parade. Men of**

forty always looked fifty and the majority had so few teeth it sometimes seemed that there was only one tooth in the entire prison and it was passed around from cell to cell on a rota basis.

Calories came as starch, and starch made the pale skins and the useless fat that have become the expensive symbols of Western poverty.

The younger men wanted to preserve their physical appearance and, conscious of the need to keep fit in case of trouble, spent every hour they were allowed in the gym. The Dartmoor gym was well equipped and manned by generous-spirited and respected instructors who rode their bikes into work over the wind and the rain of the moor.

Despite the fact that prisoners were occasionally caught taking steroids, and selling them to each other, the gym was central to the stability of both the mental and physical health of a large portion of the population. It was, literally, the pumping heart of the place.

Prisoners saved up for proteins from the canteen and they bulked up, talking to each other about muscle density and bench presses. It was good to be big, 'hench', as it was known. Tattooed and hench, that was the look. 'Don't even try it, mate' was the subtext. "My muscles are my weapons," except that in most cases, when it came down to it, muscles weren't the only weapons; weapons were the weapons. When an assault was recorded there was usually a search for whatever blunt objects had been thrown out the window or onto the roof. People who had seen it described it as 'like rain'.

Somehow, despite a man bleeding to death on the floor of the kitchen, tea had gone ahead and 600 hot meals had been served. Nobody quite knew how. But it was a good thing, as anyone with any knowledge of prison history knows, food is inextricably linked to eruptions of violence, and often one of the reasons for riots cited by roof-top protesters past and present. Governors knew they had to get the food right. Some even claimed that they ate it themselves.

'Do you think the murder will be on the telly, Miss?'

'I would be surprised if it was national news,' I said. 'The local media will get it when the police have informed the family of the victim.'

The morning carried on, slow and unsure.

Ray, who had shaken his crying baby to death, was the first to worry about the lunchtime sandwiches being contaminated with blood.

Mike, who was in for violence and wrote poetry, speculated in a loud Welsh accent about the panorama of possibilities represented by food being delivered in the event that the kitchen could not be used.

The kitchen, everyone agreed, was a crime scene; the police had probably put tape up, would there be a chalk outline on the floor? Fingerprinting? The guys who had been witnesses, 30 or so according to the rumour at that hour, had all been kept in the kitchen by the police. They had been seen returning to their cells very late at night. By the end of the session Mike was convinced that there would be Domino's pizzas. Or even MacDonald's. 600 Big Macs. Imagine. He was good at imagining things, despite having some pronounced cognitive impairment. When asked to rename the seven dwarves he had come up with Asbo and Shifty.

I checked in with the neighbouring workshop. The instructor said they would go back to their cells early.

The direction had come over the radio – movement would be at 10.45 rather than 11.45.

'How are your lot?' he asked.

'Talking about the food,' I said. 'They think they're going to get chips.'

## 3. MATCHSTICK MEN

The long morning dragged slowly on.

Ted and Alex sat in the art room sticking matchsticks onto cardboard templates with PVA glue. Ted was making a frame for a photograph of his three-year-old son. He showed me the picture of the child.

'Christ, Ted,' I said, 'that is a huge baby.'

'Yeah,' he agreed, 'the mother's a bit of a lump n' all.'

The mother had become pregnant after a one-night stand when he was 16. She hadn't been sure whose child it was until, during one of his brief periods out of prison, they had had a paternity test. Ted, in his early twenties, had the confused expression of a man who has been mugged.

Ted and Alex had come to do 'hobbies' in the informal art group I had started because there was a demand for it.

I had wanted it to be a craft enterprise, full of animals made out of cardboard and here's one I made earlier and all saleable. I saw mobiles made out of rubbish and *pâpier maché* and neat wooden toys with whirling wheels that could go on sale in the prison museum where the public liked to buy things made by actual prisoners.

My visions, however, always conflicted with the dark miasma that was the reality of prison life where the obstacles were as unpredictable as they were inevitable.

Prisoners enjoyed making models out of matches for the same reason that people like any simple tasks that centre the spirit and ease the mind. 'Matching' was meditative and interactive and the men who asked to do it always cited the anxiety of bang up as a reason. 'Sitting in me cell all day,' was a typical note handwritten on an application form. 'I have a lot time left . . . when I'm banged up I get stressed and think of bad things . . . hopefully this can take my mind off the problems I have ...'

Prison craft has an interesting history and method, its embedded longevity being a testament to the welcome fact that it is almost impossible to suffocate imagination, dexterity and acumen. As the French prisoners of Dartmoor's past used human hair to make the rigging on complex frigates, and bone to make a detailed guillotine, a prisoner of the present had made a fully working guitar out of an electric fan.

The aesthetic, both historical and current, was entirely informed by lack of materials and the need to make things from detritus with tools that were allowed. A prisoner once gave me the stub of a pencil that had been used to its last inch. 'You should frame that and call it "prison resources",' he said.

Scissors weren't allowed, neither were needles, sewing or knitting. Oil paints weren't allowed, so prisoners painted with water colour and acrylic and, if they couldn't get those, they dyed their work with tea and coffee, painted it with a mixture of coffee whitener and water, and improvised with paper clips, beads made out of rolled-up magazines and that eternal item, the scavenged loo roll.

Models were made out of the squashed-up white bread from tea that, moulded into a dough, hardened into anything from a rose to an insect. These, often brilliant, pieces of work were then painted with acrylic paint and mounted using materials usually pilfered by a mate from recycling.

Matching had to be done with safety cutters of a useless standard because the more effective model had been (unsurprisingly) banned by the prison after a prisoner (subsequently described as a 'grass' and a 'pillock') removed its blade and showed a senior governor how it could be made into a weapon.

Ted and Alex both agreed that one murder did not make Dartmoor the worst nick they had ever been in, and they had both been in several. They were both in their twenties and both in for violence. Bristol and Exeter were much worse than Dartmoor, they said. In Bristol Ted had seen a man stabbed with a Biro.

'Do you think it was to do with integration, Miss?' Ted wondered.

'I don't know,' I said. 'I don't think we know anything for sure at this point.'

'Integration' was a prison word used to describe the act of compelling prisoners from the 'main' population to live with those who had been labelled 'vulnerable' or VPs. VPs were usually, but not always, sex offenders. Sometimes, as Dan was delighted to point out, they were policemen.

In terms of prison culture, integration was huge – nonce hatred being historical, endemic and dangerous.

Some establishments over-rode the problem by confining the population solely to sex offenders (HMP Bure, in Norfolk, or instance). Dartmoor, however, had had to provide facilities to two different warring factions that had to be kept separate at all costs. The 'vulnerable' prisoners moved around the corridors as one group and the 'main' prisoners as another, separately and at different times, so they did not meet, because to meet was to fight. If you didn't fight the nonces you were a nonce yourself. That was the logic, but it was their logic, and one to which I had refused to subscribe, despite criticism from the likes of Colin who was always accusing me of 'sucking up to the bacons'.

'Look. Colin,' I would say. 'I couldn't, wouldn't and shouldn't be working in a prison if I had a problem working with sex offenders. They have been judged; I don't have to. I work with the person not the crime.'

So the two populations had different jobs, classes, courses, wings, and library times, which was patently nonsensical in terms of ever-dwindling resources. Split regimes, apart from being expensive, also, strangely, encouraged the very problems they were designed to combat, as prisoners fell into self-styled micro-societies compelled to protect each other and eternally persecute the opposition, even if, as individuals, they didn't always want to.

The new Number One Governor, Bridie Oakes-Richards, had introduced integration when she arrived in the prison in January 2015.

There had been aggro at first, especially on G Wing, but compacts had been signed, penalties for violence handed out, and the 'non-compliant' had been shipped to other prisons via the Segregation Unit.

Integration had happened and the governors were proud of that.

At 10 a.m. a message came through on the radio. The morning's education and activities were to be cut short. Everyone had to go back to their cells.

'Attention all staff. Movement will be at 10.45, I repeat at 10.45.'

'Movement' was the designated time that crowds of prisoners walked around the prison as a wave, ushered by prison officers, counted, searched, jostling, yelling at each other and making jokes about how much Mr So and So enjoyed patting them down. It was amongst the many moments that the prison was exactly like a school and it was similarly jocular; one watched individuals laughing as if they were coming back from a football match rather than being pushed towards a cell. They didn't have the sad shuffle of the oppressed and starving, the walking shadows of prison estates then and now, they were robust spirits enjoying their rare few minutes of fresh air and light.

The men went back to their wings and the staff ambled towards the chapel for a meeting to discuss what had happened in the kitchen. I didn't go. I didn't want to, and I didn't know how to, process the confused misery precipitated by this stranger's sudden death in a crowd of people I didn't know very well. The uniformed officers had each other and they were the ones that needed the support, being on the front line and in the most danger. They had to live with the actuality of the effects on the lives of the 600 men whose welfare they were attempting to supervise. I did not. I only had to stay unfrightened and positive for long enough to make regular and confident contributions.

I could flee to the outside world and attempt to think things through and then let them go.

Death, however, was walking close and there was a lot to think about, not least the unnerving coincidence that this murder had occurred on exactly the same date that I had nearly died a year earlier, a date I had come to think of as my Death Day as opposed to my Birth Day. An aneurism on November 26 2014 would have killed me if not for an emergency brain operation at Derriford Hospital in Plymouth. I wasn't particularly 'spooked' by this coincidence but, certainly, over subsequent months, I worried about the profuse and intangible experiences of prison life and the unfathomable dramas that continually played out in this walled up and isolated community.

Outside the community, in the wide world that made so little difference, various agencies and reporters were repeating statistics that showed a shaming escalation of violence both in prisoners harming each other and prison officers being assaulted. Far away from Dartmoor, in the London offices of prison inspectors and prison ombudsmen, the alarm bells had been clanging for months, warning about the disastrous decisions to cut the numbers of prison staff and issuing reports about 'unacceptably high self-inflicted deaths'.

Homicides were at a 30 year high, with eight being suspected in 2015, the highest since records began in 1978 when the previous record was five. Of the eighty-eight suicides committed in prisons in 2015, Oliver Pascoe's corpse was the one found in Dartmoor.

Oliver Pascoe didn't act out before he died. He simply hanged himself in his cell on G Wing on a Sunday night in March. He was twenty-three. I'll repeat that. He was twenty-three.

He had been imprisoned for holding a knife to various innocent throats and demanding, in one case, £20.

During the same month that Oliver Pascoe died a Mr Humphries serving a sentence at HMP Wayland wrote to the Mailbag section of *Inside Time*, the prisoners' widely distributed newspaper, and pointed out that suicide was a personal choice. 'I don't want to take my own life,' he warned, 'but I am free to do so if I want to.'

Self-death and self-harm are easy to see as amongst the few freedoms a prisoner has, as the history of incarcerated law-breakers has long proven. Amongst hunger strikers and dirty protesters the freedom to self-harm is a freedom of expression for those who feel they cannot be heard.

Oliver Pascoe's desperation had slipped under the radar. His mental health issues had been flagged up by his solicitor during his trial and were doubtless regarded as the unreliable mitigating circumstances of defence strategy, in the event that they were regarded. He was found when the cells were unlocked in the morning. He was quietly determined, as so many successful suicides are. Alone and anonymous, his decision could not be controlled by procedural coda, by OASYs or PNOMIS, or any of the other documents of accountability.

The Number One Governor distributed a notice describing the 'tragedy' and outlining an 'action plan' for recovery and improvement. People who had met Pascoe said he couldn't see particularly well, but there had been none of the usual signs of severe distress. Six guys were shipped out. The prisoners said bullying had been involved. There was speculation that he had been chucked by his girlfriend but nobody had really known him. His parents visited his cell after it had been repainted.

Leon was not (overtly) suicidal but he was dying. He appeared and reappeared in the creative writing sessions. His first action was to throw a spider at Colin, who was furious and went on and on about it, alone though he was in his fury, as everyone else laughed themselves stupid.

Small, yellow and very weak, Leon's health deteriorated until he could hardly speak. His voice was low and breathless. He was slowly dying; at the age of twenty-eight he was dying on the wing, in prison and in front of everyone, some of whom realised this and some who did not. Leon realised it; he had had a visit. 'A man come and see me from the end of life,' he said. 'I have now been told that I can't have a liver transplant and they don't know how long I've got left.'

The National Offender Management Service required a dying prisoner to be 'risk assessed' and estimated to have 'three months or less to live' before they were granted, 'compassionate release.' Nobody could tell Leon when, exactly, he was going to die, this prognosis being somewhat mystical in its elements, so he was stuck in limbo in pain and on the wing in a bureaucrat's death row.

He had a congenital chronic liver disease named autoimmune hepatitis, which meant a lot of drugs, jabs, stomach problems, breathing problems, and the insurmountable fatigue that can make the sufferer of liver disease feel like the living dead.

He had spent three months in Derriford Hospital in Plymouth, chained to a prison officer in the procedure known as 'bedwatch', which is expensive and undermines the thin resources of the regime to the extent that it can directly impact the time that the other prisoners are allowed out of their cells. Bedwatch means more bang up and it only takes one person to be in hospital.

Leon's crime, sinister and inexplicable, had been to falsely accuse a charity worker of rape in an incident that had ruined the latter's life and resulted in the closure of the charity.

He was not endearing. He smelled of the garlic he was using as a supplement, his eyes were small, blue and close together, his head was shaved, his skin was yellow, his interlocution was pretty much reduced to a low monotone nasal whining, but, like many chronically ill people, it is difficult to see the personality when the disease has subsumed it.

He was looked after with unquestioning compassion by his boyfriend who, aged twenty-five, was in for violence but was in fact attentive and loyal in the face of a challenge that asked for complete co-dependence and not a small amount of patience and courage.

There wasn't much sympathy for Leon. A prison officer reported him when he caught him taking the drip out of his arm in the loo and using the small drops of blood to make it look as if he was urinating it. The other prisoners claimed that the reason he was in that state was because he had sold the drugs he had been prescribed on the wing. He had coughed up blood in one of my creative writing sessions, so I took him very seriously.

Swimming out of my depth in the dark waters of his demise, I listened to the description of worsening symptoms, his teeth (rather good) were falling out; the pain in his legs, the fact that he wanted a Whitney Houston track to be played at his funeral. There was nothing I could do except hope that he would be allowed out to die comfortably.

Dan wrote about death after he saw a man collapse in the gym. The other prisoner had been right in front of him, working out, and had dropped hard to the ground. His life was saved by two other prisoners, gym orderlies, who resuscitated him. It had been awful and he wrote thus;

We live to linger longer, we strive to survive. But why? What is this obligatory obsession with omnipotence? Why is the Grim Reaper always the bad guy? No one who's ever met him has a bad word to say about him, so it's well within the plausibility of possibility that he's alright for a faceless guy with a scythe. Yet we forever fear the unknown, for we cannot fathom its fortunes. We are afraid. But what are we so afraid of about what we perceive to be the end? Well, we believe what we perceive. To perceive is perception, and it's perception that presents the predicament.

By Monday morning the man who had been murdered in the kitchen had been identified by the Plymouth Herald as thirty-seven-year-old Alexander Cusworth. He was not Polish, as the wing rumour had claimed, but British, from Stafford in fact.

In prison for Grievous Bodily Harm (GBH), he was, according to Colin, 'A crackhead innit'.

Certainly Cusworth had a history of being extremely violent. His eight-year sentence had come about following an incident in Teignmouth where he had beaten his landlord with a broomstick. The man had been found in a pool of blood and was rushed by ambulance to a hospital in Torbay. He suffered bleeding inside his skull and spent a week in an induced coma, eight days on a life-support machine and a month in hospital.

Cusworth had walked into Teignmouth police station after the attack and told the officer, 'I have just given him a good hiding because he called me a sex offender. He is lying face down on the floor and there is a lot of blood. I hope he is hurt because he called me a rapist.'

The victim had deserved it, he said, and was lucky he hadn't killed him.

Cusworth had admitted to wounding with intent to cause grievous bodily harm and had been told by the judge, 'You handed out a brutal beating with no justification at all.'

By that point Cusworth's drug and mental health issues had been identified. He had received an eight-month suspended sentence for, ironically in the light of the nature of his own death, threatening passengers on a bus with a kitchen knife.

Stafford Borough Councillor Ann Edgeller had fostered him when he was nine and legally adopted him when he was twelve. She gave an interview to a local paper; she had tried to visit him in Dartmoor that week but her car had broken down on the moor. He'd had a bad background and a bad drug habit, but he wasn't bad. There was hope. He had been doing well in Dartmoor, off the drugs apparently.

The 'tall fella', a 50-year-old prisoner named William Tolcher was, in the months following the murder, protected by the laws around judicial procedure, and little was known about him apart from a local news story describing a bizarre incident in Newquay when he and a mate had attacked a man stumbling back from the pub. The man had woken up in an alley in a pool of his own blood to find that he had been robbed of his wallet and, perhaps as importantly, his Ralph Lauren underwear.

Following the publication of events in the local newspapers, the Number One addressed her staff again and everyone gathered in the chapel.

'I want to acknowledge that things are different,' she said. 'We are a community affected by murder and, while we cannot even begin to imagine the pain and grief being currently experienced by Mr Cusworth's parents and family, we must acknowledge that many of our peers and our prisoners have been witness to a terrible act of violence.

'All of us must be calm, reflective and mindful of this fact when dealing with each other and our prisoner community. Speaking from my own experience on the impact of this murder upon me – I have gone through a whole gamut of things including: my own disbelief and shock, anger and revulsion; my own ego-driven lamenting – why me? Why Dartmoor? What harm will it do to my reputation and the improving reputation of Dartmoor? My own physical and emotional symptoms trying to attend to fear – yes, fear – of the unknown, what's to come in terms of accountability and where the buck stops. My own racing pulse, tiredness through hyper-ness and broken sleep, mind racing trying to make sense of what happened and why and how it can be prevented from happening again.

'I imagine that my anxiety is little different to your anxiety, your peer's anxiety, your prisoner anxiety: we are all now different by virtue of this terrible act of violence.

'It falls to all of us to ask questions on our community's safety, decency and security at times like this; we must feel free to question, offer solutions and make necessary changes to ensure nothing like this happens again. You should be aware that the Prisons and Probation Ombudsman, Jonathan Tickner, is in the establishment today and probably tomorrow to begin his investigations. Meanwhile we need to carry on doing the day job and doing it with confidence and with a hopeful future outlook.'

# 4. THE DAY JOB

Dartmoor prison is Victorian. Its first stone was laid in 1806 and its current collection of disconsolate structures are mutations and prefabrications that have been built and destroyed and built again into the final mystery, which is a cross between Gormenghast and an Escher drawing.

To peek through almost any of the million windows was to see varieties of inexplicable zones – peculiar sheds, odd boulders, piles of wood, a shock of hairy grass, a long white passageway smelling of illicit roll-ups and echoing with the faint rattle of wheels and distant male shouting. Then, suddenly, for no reason at all, there would be a flower bed full of glossily painted garden ornaments, big cement boots and concrete pigs. And all the while, round and round, the wire fence circled with its razor edges and the dank grey stone walls stood heavy with their obscure numbers painted in white.

Rusty metal exterior staircases wound up granite walls and stopped. A warren of indeterminate circuits could have led to the Minotaur but sometimes led to the Administration Block, where there were newish carpets and cashier windows, a vast whirring photocopier and neat piles of *Gate Lodge,* the magazine of the Prison Officers' Association in which the head-lines typically read 'Life after the Riots' and 'Bizarre Statement by the Justice Secretary'.

In the beginning, when I first arrived, I never understood how people had managed to escape when I had genuine difficulty finding the way out.

I perfected the art of marching around the corridors with a purposeful look, and became accustomed to ending up outside F Wing (also known, confusingly to the newcomer, as Fox Tor) again and again when, in fact, I was aiming for D Wing (also known as Down Tor).

An arrow pointed to A and E wings but the signs outside the wings themselves said Arch Tor and E wing was never called E wing but the RSU or the Resettlement Unit.

I would aim for the Resettlement Unit and end up in the freezing twilight zone that was the passage to D Wing, where everything was painted orange and the cold wasteland was dominated by curving wooden structures and pointless glass cubicles as if somebody had started to build a set for the Cybermen in 1973 and then got bored and wandered off.

There was no C Wing; well, there was, but it had been condemned. You could see it through the glass, dark and derelict, closed for reasons of sanitation.

Then one of the teachers offered to show me around. He looked exactly like that one in the Muppets who has a pair of glasses behind which there are no eyes and blows things up in the lab. Not Beaker, the other one – Dr Bunsen Honeydew.

He was warm and funny and helpful and nearing a retirement age which he had no intention of honouring. I followed him as he carried a bag of heavy Level 1 Maths and English papers and books up and down the metal steps between the landings on the wings in order to do something called peri-teaching. This meant delivering lessons to the prisoner by speaking through the slit in the side of the locked door of the cell – pushing the homework under the door and receiving new work the same way.

Every cell had an observation slit, or window, with a flap that opened from the outside, awarding a peeping power around which, quite rightly, there was a protocol. I copied this from observing Dr Honeydew. You couldn't just open the flap because the hapless felon could be doing anything and privacy is a simple thing for the outsider to honour.

So the etiquette was to knock on the door like Sheldon in *The Big Bang Theory*, introduce yourself in a loud voice, and ask permission to open the flap.

'Hello, Mr A, this is Jessica, the Writer in Residence; you sent me a General Application.'

If there was silence it was because they were 1. Asleep. 2. Did not wish to speak to anyone. 3. Deafened by thumping pop music 4. Out of the cell and wheeling the recycling bins around the corridors and then jumping on them so to see how fast they could go.

The flap could reveal a naked career criminal involved in his ablutions, amongst other things, but it also provided a picture of what was inside the cell. I was shocked to note that in the cells on G5, which were tiny, the prisoner slept with his face pointing to the loo, which was a foot away.

Colin, in a creative writing session, described what he saw when he woke up.

I see a little square box called a television. I see prison bedding which nearly always consists of thin green sheets and cross-hatched orange acrylic blankets. I see a wall of pictures and photos, people I know personally and others I don't.

In Dartmoor you are generally woken up by rays of light or in some cases full blown daytime at 5 or 6 in the morning as curtains aren't allowed here. The white china toilet with its black seat is always the same – two foot from the end of my bed. I'm sure it carries smells from other people using it. The window is about six foot off the ground, it has a mesh on the outside and, as an extra precaution, we have stoppers on the windows (kinda like door stoppers) so there's only a little crack for ventilation. A typical letterbox, I would say, is three or four times bigger than the window's ventilation.

We have a little lockable locker which is the size of a portable fridge, a bigger locker which is slimmer but not so different to a chest of drawers and a table which could be described as a glorified coffee table. A stereo was present before I broke it.

The cell is in a pretty dilapidated condition, that's not entirely my fault as it has had years of abuse, but I probably haven't helped.

When I wake up in the morning I prefer to keep my eyes closed for a little while longer so the reality of my existence doesn't hit me at least for a few moments.

When I arrived, in 2012, the Education Department was more overcrowded than the wings and conditions had turned the twenty or so teachers into a volatile pack circling around in an endless and aggressive game of musical chairs where there was no music and no chairs. Or not nearly enough chairs. Or tables. Or computers. Or paper. Or photocopying facilities. Or staplers. The rarity of the stapler and the local value therein was my first step to understanding the idiosyncratic currency of the prison system. I bought My Own in with my name painted in Tippex.

Mobs of cardigans struggled to get to the electric kettle, elbowed each other out of the way to reach their pigeon holes, waited in line for the microwave, waited for someone to hand over the milk, squashed up against each other in the few corner seats, picked at salads with the obligatory risk-assessed plastic cutlery and fanned themselves in an unbelievable heat that nobody knew how to reduce and which would have promoted the growth of an orchid.

There was one outside telephone line; internet access was limited to the Ministry of Justice website, and an expensive colour printer hadn't worked for a year because nobody knew who owned it, who had paid for it, let alone where the paperwork was – and even if all that had been retrieved requisition orders had to be signed by budget holders processed through someone called Dave (but not necessarily, it could be Paul) and then go somewhere to produce a correctly vetted and appropriate engineer who would have to be let in to the prison by people who hadn't been told who he was or why he was there.

The noise level, very high, was a sonic vocal battle where the Scots and Geordie accents triumphed by many decibels.

There was a severe shortage of paper and a teacher sacked one of his pupils when he saw him stealing it. The thief had been in the middle of a creative writing course, so I went to find him on his wing. This was not as easy as it sounds. All prisoners are allocated a 'location' such as D-203 – this means they are on

D Wing on the second landing in cell number 3. Such an address can mean a one in one climb up several flights of glossy yellow metal steps and some minutes establishing which landing you are on. D2 is not necessarily above D1 – D1 could be anywhere, so could D5; it all goes up and up and up and then suddenly, for no reason, to some 'super-enhanced' bit – and, if the prison is in 'patrol' state (meaning it is dark and everyone is asleep) it means marching up and down the spur and squinting at the sinister photographs on the outside of the cell doors depicting the various inhabitants until you find the so called address – and this might be wrong anyway, as he could have either moved cells or wings or have been transferred out. This means returning to the education department, through several corridors, a yard, rain on the head and eight locks, to find the 'Alpha List' that updates locations on a daily basis to reflect the relentless and undermining 'churn'.

The young shameless person was smiley and spotted and articulate and obsessed with nanotechnology. He was writing a (very long) novel in pencil about Lizard People – with detailed maps of the locations where they lived – and he had just finished reading *Do Androids Dream of Electric Sheep*?

He ended up in 'Gnomes' (as the concrete workshop was known) but didn't seem to mind sitting on a bench with the lads painting stone statues in the form of hedgehogs, Buddhas and country cottages. I told him not to waste his able brain, which I know he took to heart because he repeated it to the chaplain. He went out and came back in again about six months later. Burglary. 'Yeah, I know it was stupid, Jess.'

In the staff room the names of the prisoners who had been identified by the security department as being a danger to female staff were obscured in a red file underneath a bowl of bananas and a pile of *Good Housekeeping* magazines. This list was out of date and hidden by clutter but, once unearthed, provided a description of those prisoners whose records showed a wide variety of intentions. These ranged from inappropriate comments and touching; intimidating and manipulative behaviour; hostage taking; threatening POT and throwing a television set. Then there was exposing, following, rubbing, records of indecent assault and, in one case, a 'MAPPA Level 3 assessment that suggested he should be detained at Rampton Hospital.'

Later, in the quest for what the prison service called 'organisational effectiveness', the red file was rationalised with a label entitled 'Active Alerts'. Here prisoners were defined with one word against their names: Racist; Violent; Arsonist; Bully; Risk to Females; Risk to Public; Staff Assaulter.

An old 'staff observation' book, where teachers made handwritten notes about the learners, described incidents that were more reflective of aggressive adolescents than predatory assailants.

*SIR (Security Incident Report) completed as Mr S asked me what I would do if he held a gun to my head.*

*Verbal warning given to Mr A for using inappropriate language (wee-wee and poo-poo).*

*Mr A tore up his exam paper and said stick it up your fucking arse.*

*Mr S tore up contents of his art folder, called a tutor a racist and loudly slammed door.*

*Racist graffiti written on windowsill – Kill all Muslims. Fuck Allah.*

*Mr L refused reasonable request to put puzzle away, continued to argue and become abusive to staff. Alarm pulled.*

*Mr S is in a very bad mood.*

*Mr H informs me that he suffers from schizophrenia and can hear voices.*

Mr C arrived at a writing session talking to himself and carrying a polythene bag in which there was a half-eaten sandwich and a TV remote control. Then he turned his back on the group and shouted, 'I CAME ALL OVER HER FACE!'

This went on for a couple of days. I was new, assisting a teacher, and had little confidence in my own judgement, but Mr C clearly had mental health issues and was building up to an episode. Unpleasant and unnerving though his aggression was, he hardly knew where he was.

The teacher handed me a yellow 'Post-It' with the man's name on and whispered to go to the staff room and request an escort to take Mr C back to his wing.

A chubby young officer in his twenties arrived and there was a struggle. He placed Mr C in a restraining position – face down on the desk, arms behind his back – and told the teacher to push the green alarm button.

There was a long three minutes while everyone stared in silence at this slow motion scenario, as Mr C lay flat on the desk with the young officer on top of him, then, incredibly excitingly, about eight uniformed officers arrived and the room was full of cavalry.

The decision as to where to place the non-complier was complicated by the fact that nobody (including him) knew which wing he was on and there was no room in 'Seg' or the Security Care and Control Unit (SCCU) as it is officially entitled because it was already full.

Several officers asked if I was OK and one officer held up a broken plastic knife as if it was a three-foot sabre – assuming it to be evidence of dangerous intent. Then everyone disappeared to write the innumerable 'incident report' forms.

The teacher of the class was shaken and said that it was the first time in several years of experience that he had pressed the green alarm bell.

'Classes', known as sessions, were three hours long. I began by sitting in on the classes taught by experienced teachers in order to learn the esoteric skill set demanded by groups of adult learners of all ages and backgrounds whose disparity defied any cohesive outcome. This was not a normal classroom, despite the fact that interminable education agencies judged it as one.

Teachers on the frontline danced to the tune of an unseen network of managers who had never been in a prison and could not possibly know the exact nature of either the learners or the environment that impacted their 'learning experience'.

The young father of three, for instance, who transferred to HMP Dartmoor with qualifications in Forklift Driving (including counterbalance and reach) and a Level 3 certificate from the British Institute of Cleaning Science (including hazardous waste) was also the person who wrote that his 'farther was a violent alcoholic' and his foster mother, 'assaulted me with a peace of wood and a High-hill shoe.'

There could be a fat Rasta with a West Country accent who monopolised a class by doing long and boring card tricks. There could be a Mohawk with a ring through his nose who liked the author Danny Wallace, and a monosyllabic youth who, asked to write the first part of his autobiography, wrote about the car accident in which he was driving and his best friend died.

There could be several people leaving in the middle of the session to get their methadone, and there could be Stan who, influenced by the comedian Noel Fielding (of surreal comedy series *The Mighty Boosh*) had died his big hair scarlet and yellow, an arrangement that he described as his 'Boosh', as in, 'Oi. Don't knock the Boosh.'

He had been employed by a local authority as an ethical hacker (a computer expert who helps defend an organisation against hacking). They then fired him so he hacked in and stole some money.

He was unafraid to admit that he had a Buzz Lightyear outfit and was obsessed by Land Rovers. His written work – elucidating journalistic assignments on paper – was hampered by the fact that he had only ever communicated through the medium of the computer programme. 'I speak five languages in that,' he explained. So he couldn't spell – unless the computer did it for him – or punctuate.

Defining himself as a subversive, he came under some suspicion when a sign mysteriously emerged from Room 2's printer saying 'Fuck the Police' in an 18-point Gothic font. It could have been any one of a dozen men, as the Room 2 printer was connected to a number of computers in different classrooms, but Stan giggled about it, a lot, which set me off, of course.

Danny was content to stare lethargically at an old edition of the *Daily Mirror*, having claimed that he was not supposed to be in Creative Writing anyway, or anywhere in the education department, but was stuck there if he did not wish to receive an 'IEP' – a piece of paper that could result in a prisoner being demoted from a Standard to a Basic regime, which meant, amongst other things, that their television was taken away.

Danny had managed to dodge the IEP but he didn't have as much luck with the IPP, (Indeterminate Sentence for Public Protection) with which, at the age of twenty-four, he had been sentenced.

Typically an IPP was given to a person who had committed violent acts and whose release relied on his completing various offending behaviour courses. These offending behaviour courses were rarely available, meaning that the prisoner could not prove to the probation service, or anyone else, that he was no longer a 'risk', meaning that he had to stay in prison and serve a sentence way beyond what his release date should have been.

The IPP was introduced in 2005, by the then Home Secretary David Blunkett, and revoked in 2012 following protest from almost every important agency involved in the criminal justice system and a case brought against the Secretary of State for Justice which was upheld by the European Court of Human Rights. It was estimated that 6,000 lives, many of them very young, had been adversely affected at great expense to both the individual and the tax-payer.

It was impossible to tell what Danny had done to incur such a term. The only clues were a dominant interest in Manchester City and some terrible white scars on the inside of his arm that could have signified self-harm or a bad fight. He said he could read but he could not spell.

'Is there anything that you know you are good at?'

'Nothing, Miss – I didn't go to school. I just sit in me cell.'

That week Dedryck Boyata, the Belgian footballer and then defender for Manchester City, had kicked an Arsenal player in the head and the tabloid photograph looked as if the assault was deliberate. The £20 million acquisition was sent off. This behaviour was genuinely shocking to Danny, who couldn't understand how somebody with that much money and talent could behave like that. (Boyata received a red card, though management complained at the time, saying he was a good lad and it was a mis-timed tackle.)

By the end of the 'one to one' we had read the various newspaper reports so I knew a bit about Manchester City, and Danny knew how finance turned into financially and nation turned into nationally and that they weren't spelled *nashnully* and *finanshully* – even if they should be. 'The English language is ridiculous and nobody knows how to spell it properly,' I said, neither for the first or last time during the residency.

'You aren't stupid – you can learn; look what you've done in just an hour.'

Later I tried to find Danny, having bought a football magazine suitable for practising his reading. His cell door was half open and the cell was dark. I knocked and called but there was no answer. Several weeks later I saw him cleaning the corridors in order to avail himself of a qualification from the British Institute of Cleaning Science (BICS). He looked much happier.

'My brother's coming, Miss.'

'To visit?'

'Nah, to me wing – he's in the prison.'

One man told me he was doing 'Creative Writing' classes because, 'I've done everything else.' This was his seventh year in prison; he had arrived at the age of nineteen in a wheelchair, having been shot in the leg during a gang fight in Brixton. He revealed this fact with the smirk of a man for whom the history of rap began with Tupac Shakur and who, it turned out, had never heard of the Sugar Hill Gang.

He asked if I would help him promote his rap. I said people in the business would not take any notice of the opinion of a white middle-aged middle-class woman on this subject.

Tyrone, not known for either listening or taking no for an answer, made the good point that that was exactly why people would listen to me, because if he moved me it meant he was good because I was an outsider and not part of the culture.

The problem was that neither Tyrone nor his creative work did move me. He irritated me. And I was not alone – he was very good-looking and coldly self-serving – and the other female teachers found him creepy, the way he followed them around and stood in their space and insinuated that they fancied him so much they found it difficult to control themselves.

He did have a sense of humour, of a kind; he was always making jokes about my voice and glasses; however he was disliked by the brothers on the wing (a garrulous group who tended to sit in a corner playing cards and entertaining themselves with the countermands of fraternal banter) because of his inclination to play the race card at the drop of a hat and for no good reason. They knew that to overplay the race card was to undermine its effect when it was actually needed and they were right.

Tyrone was a shouter; you get them in places where there is a lot of testosterone and everyone wants attention. He delivered long loud monologues of opinion about the fact that prison wages were slavery; about how the system held his career back because reception wouldn't let him have his tapes from his property box; about how he was too clever for this class that he could should be doing Level 3, why wasn't he doing Level 3? They were holding him back because he was black.

He started his debates like fires, not because he was interested in discourse, but because he wanted control over the audience. The rest of the group didn't need much ignition to light the 'Dartmoor is a Joke' fulmination.

His fiery depositions were, however, undermined by the fact that they were not fuelled by information. He had no ability (or desire) to support his points or to elucidate. When challenged he had a tantrum. When I told him that I found all this intimidating to me and disruptive to the rest of the class he countered that I should respect the cultural difference – that is how black people speak, he said, loudly and argumentatively. I agreed with this, having lived in Brixton for two years, but I was bored of being asked to accept bullying as a cultural concept. I said I didn't realise he was black, at which point he flounced out of the classroom and reported my racism all over the wing.

Altercations are very undermining when they occur in a picture where a woman is quite often alone in a class of men charged with violent and/or sexual offences. When a vibrating hooligan shouts in your face it is extremely difficult to know the best form of defence because the base line could be a violent assault from which you cannot defend yourself. They may not actually hit you, but they can make life very unpleasant, and when one starts shouting at you, at least two others will joyfully join in.

The reasoned argument is the only method of defence and, though the debate might (and usually does) resolve itself and the prisoner will occasionally apologise,

('Sorry, Miss. I was out of order. I think it was because I'm givin' up smoking'), it reduced the confidence and slowed down the work. I would make less effort over the next couple of days, and stop caring. It was insidious and it was what nearly every prison employee experienced on a day-to-day basis.

I was fortunate that one of the first people I worked with was a considerate and aspirational Australian. Calm through regular Buddhist sessions in the chapel – and clever – he was writing stories for his children, from whom he had been separated for many months having received a seven-year sentence for growing cannabis on a commercial level, which he had cultivated in the hope of using the money to take himself and his young family back to Australia. The irony was that having been arrested for this operation the government then paid him to go back to Australia, so he achieved his goal anyway.

'Is this your first time on the wing?' he asked

'Yes,' I said, wondering if it was that obvious.

I was nervous and my heart was beating, as would that of any lone woman wondering amongst hundreds of stateless pirates, tattooed and bulked up in the gym, who tended to shout rather than speak (due to the acoustics on the wings) and against whom one had no defence at all.

'You know it's at your own risk,' the landing officer commented when I wrote down my name in crayon in the 'wing visits' book, a motley scrap of paper with no identifiable date.

The instructions for one to one meetings with prisoners were explicit —do not go into their cell, ensure you meet in a room with an alarm button, and some unclear advice about backs to the wall, although I could never remember the specifics of this; couldn't remember whose back was supposed to be where.

The Australian gentleman, luckily for me, was your run-of-the-mill pothead. His story had begun in a farming village in West Australia where, 'sheep out-number the human population by ten to one.' He and his three siblings were raised by their mother, on welfare. Having no future in the area he joined the army, after which he settled in South London with a large group of squatters and busked in the tube stations to earn money. Falling into the London-based sound system culture he worked as a DJ, playing reggae and jungle all over the world, finding work as crew at live music events and festivals. We met for several sessions where we discussed his short stories .He spoke about his love for his children and his need to improve his reading and writing.

Trevor Browne was the second prisoner who requested a 'one to one' session with the Writer in

Residence. He was described to me by one of the teachers as 'poor little thing he's only got one eye.' She said, 'He's written his life story – he needs a scribe.'

I met him in the classroom on F Wing where a prison officer who knew his family informed me that Browne was a drug dealer involved with underage girls and had ruined his mother's life.

'Don't waste your time,' he advised. 'He's a waste of space.'

The prison officer's opinion was supported by the local newspaper report that featured Browne's face on the cover with his son and the headline 'Row over £10 led to vicious gang beating for student.'

Browne pleaded guilty (eventually) to stabbing a Spanish student in the stomach with a ten-inch blade. His 'previous' included wounding with intent, possession of a bladed article, and two counts of battery.

The account of Trevor's story on a local newspaper's website had received various comments from members of the public:

*'How many times are they going to let the strange-looking freak stab people before he kills someone?'*
*'Pathetic and gross.'*
*'All for ten pounds – what causes that severe stupidity and mindless thuggery?'*
*'Doesn't the editor realise that sex sells newspapers? Look at the other front pages on the newsstand. No one will buy a paper with these three pictured on the front.'*

Trevor Browne was small and round, aged about forty, with dark-brown hair cut into a pudding bowl helmet and chopped into an uneven crenellation at the top of his forehead. His grey tracksuit seemed to be hanging onto his various protuberances for dear life. One yellow tooth stood in the middle of his mouth; one brown eye stared wildly out to the left. But man could he talk.

Hostage-taking can assume many forms and speaking a non-stop nonsensical monologue is one of them. Ensuring that there was a desk between us, I listened as he skipped around and around anecdotes of surreal absurdity that allowed neither interruption, clarification or interrogation.

'I done everything, Jess . . . smuggled tortoises from Wally in Tunisia and sold them for two-hundred quid, though two died . . . took a thousand space-cakes to Reading . . . did a community sentence burning gorse bushes . . . me second wife was a prostitute out the windows in Amsterdam . . . I can make hooch out of Marmite, sugar and water . . . done a still, make the steam out me kettle . . .'

I met him for several writing sessions in an effort to identify any elements of truth, record what he was trying to say, and aid its elucidation. His main reason for requiring this provision was based on his prediction of an early death.

'I want it written down before I die, Jess.'

My reason? I was meandering in an intervention pathway to find a key that might unlock some hidden potential or illuminate a truth that would be useful to this weird recidivist. Although I became less sympathetic as time went on, I began with a man whose primary problem was a long-term addiction to drugs, as was apparent in his handwritten life story which was beginning to take shape on cheap, lined paper.

I was close to my parents, and they would come around in the car and take us out for a drink. We would go out in the country. They could not understand why I would always have my eyes closed. I would drift off into my own little dream world and only come around when Alison would give a sharp dig with her elbow ... they just couldn't understand it and that was fine by me. I was in the world I wanted to be. I thought this is how it should be, everything was wonderful. I didn't know it at the time, but I would end up with nothing. Hindsight? I never knew the meaning of this word and even if I did I would have said to myself fuck it.

**He wrote as he spoke, as was evinced by an account of his twenties.**

After yet another short stay in jail I was back at my bedsit, my boy was only young, just a baby, he didn't really understand where I had been or why and maybe it was best that way.

'Right,' I said to my girl, 'since I've been away all has not been lost, love. I've been hanging about in the prison with a German guy and he has been telling me how we could go about earning us some extra cash.'

My girl knew me well by now. We had moved into our own little bedsit, she was only sixteen at the time, she would have known that I didn't mean I had got myself a job sorted out, no, hard work didn't really fit in with my lifestyle unless it was ripping a house apart to get at all the scrap metal.'

**Following several sessions of these anecdotes, I arrived in the staff room of the Education Department to find a note in my pigeon hole informing me that Trevor had been taken to 'Seg' on a dirty protest. The general opinion was that he had been taken off Subutex in Dartmoor and wanted to transfer to score.**

I went to see him in the 'Seg'. Viewing him through the oblong slit, I could see that he was surrounded by reams of handwritten notes that were due to be received by his unfortunate solicitor. He asked me, with characteristic eccentricity, to bring him a book on the B'ahai faith.

Later I saw him being wheeled around the corridor in a wheelchair waving and looking pleased with himself, but he was transferred out before I could find out why.

# 5. LIFE ON THE WING

F Wing was considered to be a 'nice' wing.

There was a garden outside in which various ferrets were housed. Reg and Ron arrived in a bag with somebody's missus and were granted permission to enter the prison in order to intimidate the embarrassing rat population. The famously disgusting scent of the ferret deters the rats and the two mustelids were walked around the prison on leads, occasionally making a break for it and reappearing at inopportune moments, as if they were in a sit-com, leaping out of gym cupboards and so on.

While Mike and his brother Keith (members of a criminal biker gang) smoked roll-ups in the garden and conspired to implement an ambitious breeding programme, one of the senior governors augmented the scene with the adoption of 'Gareth' from the Woodside Animal Welfare Trust in Plympton. This was accompanied by a front page local news story featuring a charming portrait of governor and Gareth, photographed through prison bars, and explaining that the animal sanctuary were quite keen to get rid of Gareth on account of his violent personality. There had been problems adopting other ferrets because Gareth tended to attack them. However, the claim was that Gareth liked people, just not ferrets, and was easy to handle once you got to know him.

Mike and Keith eventually got out of the prison and resettled. I never found out whether the ferrets managed to achieve the same outcome.

F Wing was smaller than the rest of them – two landings, about forty men, a huge communal television and efficient and personable landing officers. Prisoners had tables to eat their food with each other if they wanted to, which made the difference to the atmosphere of the evening meal. I held ' surgeries' there advertised by a hopeful notice on the door of a vacant classroom and held creative writing sessions with D who had learned to read and write in prison, G who made a Christmas card out of cardboard and glitter, and a quiet nomad with a fixed stare who told me how he would ' case' houses for some days before burgling them. His short stories were dominated by descriptions of people being dismembered in the dark with an array of automated blades.

Mr Holmes, aged seventy, on F Wing, was educated, articulate and homeless. He did not mind being homeless particularly, tough though it was. He accepted his life wandering about the countryside in the middle of the night, freezing cold, listening to badgers and trying to find a church door by which to sleep. He called it 'skippering' and was writing an autobiography about it, in long hand on lined foolscap paper, when he could get it.

## WINTER 2011
Awoke to the unusual sound of rustling then realized it was the sound of the black bin liners and bubble wrap I had used as insulation around my old sleeping bag.

Before sleep had previously encompassed me in that draughty dusty alcove of what was a disused south porch of an old church, I had listened to the local weather on my trusty little radio minus three degrees to minus five it said. When I stuck my head out I thought they had been conservative it felt a lot colder.

I had not eaten for two days having been forced out of the nearest town centre by drunken youths coming out of the pubs. I had walked miles and the only respite a drop-in centre.

There was no option but to walk and thumb. Short winter days, rain and sleet left me bedraggled. No one picks you up when you're wet. Yet another day without food. Lucky I had water. Then it began to get dark. I had to walk through the night. My little torch gave out enough light to stop me falling into the ditches.

Then I heard something on the other side of the road; a growling screaming noise, a glimpse of a white stripe, an arched back – the dim torch lit a fully grown male badger warning me off. Bloody hell! He turned his head towards me. My heart pounded. He kept his distance as he passed by, watching me as I, transfixed with fear, made sure there was at least 20 feet between us. He warned me again with a gruff growl and dived into the hedge.

My heart rate slowly came down. My focus returned. I remembered that badgers followed the same route from A to B through generations; that is why so many die on the roads. I must have crossed his regular route.

I am now absolutely starving but must keep walking. Sparkly hard frost had formed and adhered to my coat. My bleeding bag is digging into my shoulder got to keep going can't stop for fear of hypothermia. The shoulder pain takes my mind off the hunger for a while . . .

**In prison for one of his short but regular sentences, he kept his head down and appreciated the luxuries of a**

bed, warmth and regular meals. He knew his needs and had no money to buy anything; and he knew not to borrow because he knew that, 'in prison, debt can literally mean death.'

Debt and its perils were difficult to avoid in the black market that underpinned the fabric of wing life where the economy was defined by the fact that most prisoners were existing on a median wage of £8 a week to buy everything that was not the food supplied by the institution and where there was no actual cash. Barter had produced new financial life forms moulded by the consumer demand for rare commodities which could be anything from tobacco and drugs to bananas and stamps.

Nineteenth century coins excavated during work on Dartmoor prison in 1971 proved that this was ever thus. In the early days of the building's history, when it held 10,000 French prisoners of war, commerce was encouraged. An old copy of the Prison Rules states that a market was allowed to be held outside the gates from 9am to 12 noon and prisoners could sell articles of their own manufacture, except for mittens, shoes, plaited straw and 'obscene pictures'.

The current Prison Rules prohibited gambling and trade with little effect. The atmosphere on G wing on Friday afternoons was like the stockmarket after the prison officers had delivered the 'canteen' parcels of items that had been ordered from a list of groceries and paid for by the prisoners' personal accounts, known as ' spends'.

All doors were then unlocked by hand and yelling vendors clattered up and down the metal stairs. There were long souk-style negotiations about quantities, qualities and timelines for payback. Strangely prisoners were noticeably skilled at the making of sophisticated business transactions without having learned either Maths or English in the state education system.

Drug addicts on the inside, as they were on the outside, were easy but unreliable marks. They borrowed, they did not pay back, and they caused fights because they bought drugs before they bought phone credit or coffee, meaning that they either scrounged these things or stole them. Colin, quite often in debt for the above reasons, observed, 'Pad thieves are likely to be people who are already in debt. If they rob your cell you may be tempted to replace the stolen stuff by getting into debt yourself, a vicious circle.'

Prisoners argued that it was impossible to remain free of debt unless you had money of your own, or your family was supporting you. If you didn't use the telephone, didn't have a television (which cost about £1 a week) ate only the prison food, wore prison-issue clothes, found more work, and used the library, you might have a chance.

The men on F Wing were 'Enhanced', which meant that they had earned certain privileges (such as permission to own a Playstation, which they bought themselves) by conforming to the regime's demand to prove improvement by committing to schemes and jobs that helped other prisoners. Some became Listeners (trained by the Samaritans to be on call twenty-four hours a day); others became Insiders who were employed to support new arrivals into the prison.

Ahmed, a career burglar, was one of the regular attendants to the 'Writers' Surgeries' I held on F Wing. He seemed drawn to the sessions possibly because I patiently listened while he described a spectacular range of medical symptoms.

Believing that he was in real muscular pain, I wondered if he had fibromyalgia. A prison doctor prescribed him a stash of painkillers, which might well have been his intention all along. He also grew twice the size overnight, which I think was the result of a combination of steroids and carbohydrates.

He enjoyed complicated discussions about geopolitics and ended up writing an article that reflected real insight about the reason for and the development of his criminal behaviour.


## A CRITICAL POINT

My first memories go back to around the age of three years. I clearly remember my older bro's birthday and one present he received, it was a tank which to me was the dog's bollocks. I can remember watching the tank move across the floor and thinking to myself that my bro was a lucky fucker. That's it, my first emotion was of jealousy and of wanting to have things which weren't mine.

A few months later my bro was ill and getting my mum's attention. Again I clearly remember being jealous of this and I wished I were ill so I could be the centre of attention. I actually faked an illness so I could lie on the sofa with a blanket over me. Not a good start to my life I think. Perhaps if I had explained my feelings to my parents this emotion could have been dealt with in a more positive and constructive way.

Anyhow I was about six years old and my brother and I were into collecting football stickers. We both had a sticker album and for some reason I believed if I filled my album first I would be number one. This thought led me to become somewhat obsessed about getting all the stickers. Nobody knew this was my feeling and again I never dealt or asked for help with these emotions of desire, jealousy. I kept them hidden and they rolled around in me and festered, taking control of me whenever they wanted.

Anyway going back to collecting those football stickers. My father (may Allah bless him and show him mercy) was visiting relos in Pakistan. He'd left a money pouch in mum's possession with small change in it. It was a denim money belt and it had five pence and ten pence coins one side.

However on the other pocket of the belt there was an amount of copper coins. This is a point in my life that all the emotions and desires that were running around in me came to life. I can remember creeping into my mum's room and opening the cabinet door and without looking at the money bag I put my hand into one side and brought out a few pence in 5ps and 10ps. All the time I was looking straight at the bedroom door expecting my mum to catch me. However no-one came and now I had money to get these stickers.

I can remember going to the shop with my bro with our pocket money.

'One packet of stickers and some gum,' said my bro to the shopkeeper.

'10 pence please,' replied the shopkeeper and then he looked at me and asked whether I'd like the same. But oh no not today I was doing things differently. I had now begun a journey to the dark side.

'Um no I'd like 6 packets of stickers please and some penny sweets.'

The shopkeeper looked surprised but he gave me what I asked for.

On the way home my bro asked me how I had got the extra money. I confidently said I had found it and it was just pure luck.

Looking back on this situation it is now clear. I was blatantly lying and worse than that I was lying to myself. I'm saying all this because this point in my life was critical; this is the point at which I swerved off the straight route. Don't get me wrong I never swayed because I wanted to but I chose to.

'Friends?' said Alex. 'It starts with people knocking on your door asking for burn [tobacco], sugar or coffee and then leaving you alone when you tell them that you don't smoke. Then you branch out, talk to your immediate neighbours and try to gain information about the regime or work prospects. After numerous applications you gain employment and find yourself working next to people not only from your own wing but other wings too. Talk amongst yourselves starts to deviate from work and onto common interests, sports, TV etc., and you find that the time flies by faster than before.'

While some made friends, it was also possible to stay alone in your cell for months, as one man discovered. A middle-aged first timer plucked from his ordinary white collar life via offences involving webcams and 13-year-olds, he recorded his experiences in an article for the prison magazine.

**FIRST TIMER**

You're told that the top bunk is yours and that you can store your stuff under the table in the corner. You do as you're told, trying your best to be as friendly as you can be, but in reality you're a bag of nerves. Everything that is bad and could happen to you is racing through your mind. You have no idea what this other guy is in for? Am I safe?

The cell is bland, devoid of any home comforts, with a bunk bed to one side and a couple of rickety old tables and chairs. There's a basin and toilet. They look dirty. Paint peels off the walls and is that mould on the ceiling? The windows, which open barely an inch, are also grimy, too high to see through anyway.

What to do first? I look at my new bed. It consists of a thin plastic covered mattress and an equally thin pillow. It suddenly occurs to me. How do I make up my bed which is head and shoulders above me? I grab my kit removing my bedding and throwing it on to the mattress. I am already very tired.

I clamber up the casing of the bunk bed and clumsily roll myself on to the mattress, doing my best not to disturb my pad mate as he watches television.

The metal casing of the bed squeaks with every move I make. My next problem: How to make my bed whilst sitting on it and without making any noise whatsoever? Not a huge problem you may think, but after the day I have just had it was just one task too many. I simply roll myself up in a sheet and blanket, turn my back on the world and after an hour or two reviewing the worst day of my life, slowly drift off to sleep, waking every so often when I hear the slightest sound I don't recognise. It's a long night.

I awake to the clatter of the cell door opening and the thunder of multiple voices trying to make themselves heard from the wing landing outside. So it is true. I am here. Slowly, reality dawns. God help me.

My pad mate is out of the door straight away, off to see his mates and I am alone. I struggle out of my bed and make a drink. The door is open. Do I venture out? What's it like out there? What will happen to me? These thoughts and others go through my mind as I finish my drink. I draw up some courage and walk towards the door. All of my senses are at a heightened state, my mind racing as I get closer. Finally I reach the door and close it. I feel far safer in the cell. The outside world can wait for another day.

I would later come to regret that decision. Apart from when I had to leave the cell in order to eat, I kept myself to myself. Spending my time reading and writing; nothing of great importance, it was just something to pass the time. My daily routine became entrenched and I had successfully created a new bubble around my life, a safe zone. It worked so why change it? I could live like this for the foreseeable future. Easy!

However the confidence I had placed in being able to control my own sanity was eroded very quickly. Doing the same thing day in, day out, seemed like a good way to beat the system, but as time went on I longed for something new to happen

Four months passed. I had exhausted the reading material which I had brought in with me and trying to re-teach myself basic maths was a fruitless exercise.

The days were passing more slowly and I was beginning to feel it. I know now that it was loneliness that had found a strangle hold on me. Ignoring the rest of the human race was no longer going to be an option. It was the appearance of a guard at the door asking if we wanted to go to the library that finally broke the monotonous regime of my daily life.

Stepping out on to the landing, I followed the others to the library. This wasn't so bad. Why had I not done this sooner? I cursed myself for the lost opportunity. However this was a turning point for me, because in the library I found leaflets about some courses and education that the prison was running. I could do that I thought. And so, there and then I signed up.

Over time life got easier and I made some great friends. Today I enjoy getting out of my cell and interacting with others, to the point that I find myself becoming a point of reference for some who need help.

Mental health problems, profound and commonplace, tended to be addressed with anti-psychotics ( known as 'serial killers' by the prisoners) from the health team and common sense from officers, who were well used to men talking to themselves, men seeing things that weren't there, anger, paranoia, mad lying and chronic cutting.

One individual who turned up to the creative writing sessions had been hit on the head with a pool cue. He insisted, quite aggressively, that he was Darth Vader and that he was imbued with an omniscience that made him Lord of all he surveyed.

He kept blinking in the belief that when his eyes were closed he was invisible to the present, as he had transported to a parallel universe, the universe where he was Lord.

This would have been perfectly acceptable if he hadn't had a record for aggression and if these ramblings had not unsettled the other members of the group who did not know how to interact with Darth.

Darth unnerved them and incited aggressive responses, both in the members of the team and, I am ashamed to report, in myself.

'Please sit down,' I would snap, 'and let the others do their work.'

This was an inadequate response to a person who had handed in a piece of writing that expounded his belief that he had been born 'a very powerful baby boy who was to become known as Master of the Universe.'

Darth seemed to be unclear about what medication he was on, but nervous about being sectioned. The computer calmed him down, as screens do, and he sat in front of it elucidating his fantastic inner life. 'We had a family that posed as Royals. Their job was to be seen in the media to fool assassins and warlords and keep them away from HRH Master of the Universe who resided in Hampshire.'

A long-term prisoner who had observed inmates over the many years of his sentences had noticed that the 'nutjobs' were often the loudest and the most annoying people on the wings.

Which individuals during your prison sentence do you remember? The noisiest. The most oddly behaved. Those who disrupted the regime the most. In other words, the most annoying. What is unanimous about our opinion of the most annoying people? You can't wait to get rid of them. The prison reacts the same way. Problem people are bounced from wing to wing and prison to prison and the 'nuisance' tag follows on behind. I'm sure we've all heard the comment, 'he shouldn't be in prison, he should be in hospital.' We create a merry-go-round of misery that certain people can't get off from. Those people have annoying habits, but they also have specific needs which aren't met.

Coping and defence mechanisms are as individual as the personality they are protecting and it is likely that a man's behaviour will atrophy to adapt to the constant threat, lack of personal space, and lack of physical exercise.

After a discussion in a class session about how prison affects personality, a prisoner wrote an article for the prison magazine about how inmates treated each other.

In all my years of incarceration, I have found that the driving forces behind most inmates' coping mechanisms are rumour, invention and character assassination. It seems to be important that while some prisoners build themselves up, some are determined to prove that other people are not what they seem or prove that staff have some personal agenda.

Prison is essentially a social ladder. The rungs of that ladder can be defined by a variety of things including, amongst other things; the prison job a person does, their physical size, their monetary value outside the prison or even their intellect. The further up the ladder an individual can climb, the easier prison time can be or the easier it can be to get things done.

Now heaven forbid a prisoner should not be truthful but these are the answers to the average questions.

1) What sort of car do you drive? *I drive a Subaru Impreza.*
2) Can you cook? *I'm a qualified chef.*
3) What job do you do on the outside? *I earn £300 a day as a roofer.*
4) What sort of place do you live in? *I paid cash for my own house.*

Nobody ever drives a crappy little Peugeot 205, burns baked beans, gets minimum wage as a cleaner or has a nasty bedsit owned by a slum landlord. Can you blame them? Prison can be the ultimate escapism. Everyone's problems can be left at the gate, whether they're emotional, social, monetary or otherwise, and to distance yourself from them even further, why not add a little creativity to your life?

What we have to remember though, is that we are very unlikely to socialise with these people on release to our own areas, so why not indulge them on this occasion? After all, we all have our different ways of coping with prison.

Many do not cope. Mr S, for instance, was taken to healthcare where he informed them that he had taken 16 Olanzapine tablets that he had bought from another prisoner. He was taken to hospital where restraints did not prevent him from hitting himself on the head with the cuffs and repeating that he was going to kill himself and he had already said the final goodbye to his mother.

Bang up, as the caging process was known, affected different people in different ways, and some were more harmed by it than others. MedZ fed the jackdaws and wondered if they were the souls of the dead. Colin dressed up as a woman for a laugh, though it was generally agreed that he did not need much encouraging. Wandering around one heard, 'Are we on for chess, Geoff?' and discussions floating from the huddles of men sitting on each other's tiny green beds with the tiny TV flickering its coloured square in the background.

'I see Rolf Harris went straight to D Cat.'

'Yeah, in Ley'ill inny.'

'I thought it was Ford.'

'Nah, Wandsworf then Ley'ill.'

'That's fucked, man.'

'S'money innit.'

'Don't 'spect we'll be 'earing much of that 'Two Little Boys' song.'

The wings were usually clean due to the seriousness with which cleaning was taken, the time allowed for it, the job opportunity it represented and the fact that qualifications offered by the BICS (the British Institute of Cleaning Science) were embedded in the system. Indeed one prisoner, guided in the writing of his CV, was found to have had just the one job, 'cleaning in Dartmoor Prison.'

On some wings they had fish tanks with strict photocopied instructions to 'refrain from unplugging', though it was an accurate reflection of the nature of the tanks' audience that one shoal died when a prisoner lobbed bleach into the water. On purpose. The small things were often the most unnerving.

The landing office was an important interface, as it was where the prisoner would become known to the officers in charge of him. The prisoner would arrive with a black eye ('where did you get that, Russell?' 'Fell down, Boss') or the scars of recent self-harm, or a request to ring home because mum had died or Kylie was in hospital, or to complain that, 'I still 'aven't been paid, Guv.'

The landing office was sometimes an old cell, sometimes a glass-fronted receptacle containing the prison officers who were on duty to run the wing. It had their computer, various lists of the names of prisoners and where they were supposed to be, a telephone, a Tannoy system that nobody could resist doing funny voices over, shuddering plastic office in-trays (known as dip trays) pertaining to the post that was supposed to be delivered to each landing, and notices that said things like 'Manners Cost Nothing.'

The landing officers exercised a great deal of patience under challenging circumstances. An impatient insult or tetchy response takes on a wider echo within the acoustics of landing life; they can set up dangerous grudges and responses that fester and boil behind the endlessly locked doors and later erupt as a delayed outburst, although not necessarily against the same officer with whom the prisoner had, 'got the 'ump'.

Prisoners often got the 'ump, though the sensible older ones knew that the petty trivia of perceived infraction were a waste of time. As prison officers knew how to assess dangerous prisoners, prisoners learned to assess the efficient and kind officers and wait to ask them for help. Neil's relationship with his girlfriend was saved when he sent a Dear John letter to her because he had been unable to speak to her on the telephone and assumed she had dumped him. He then spoke to his girlfriend and all was well but the Dear John letter was in the post room until it was recovered by an understanding officer.

MO, who marked his fifty-eighth birthday behind bars, was an example of somebody whose inner life, though challenged by the enforced hours of boredom, was not crippled by it, largely because he had the capacity to articulate the aspects of his inner life.

## Bang up on your birthday

I wake up to the sound of a seagull, serenading me via consistent squawking. (5.45 am). It's my birthday. How come the noisy bastard knows that?? He doesn't really. He does it every bloody morning. I would chuck him some birthday cake to throw a difference into his life, but the grating in front of the four barred cell window prevents any re-distribution of prison wealth.

I make a cup of tea in my prison mug, to which I've got used to, so long as it's Typhoo. I get back into bed, prop myself up, and open up all my cards. SO THANKS, to you all, so very much for your lovely thoughts and wishes, which give me so much strength. I cry. Not a good start to the day, but what did you expect. The last time I had this many was on my Forty-ith. The kindness shown to me is such a great comfort, and I get a grip of myself again quickly, particularly when I see that some of you have sent me cash as well. Thank you so very very much. I read through all my cards and letters again and enjoy all the comments and expressions once more, with only a lump in my throat this time.

My kettle is 3 ft away, my toilet is 4 ft away, my sink is 3 ft away, and my biscuit tin is only arms' length. Sheer Bloody Luxury. I have a remote for both the TV and stereo which are unfortunately 5 ft away, and therefore, I am able to turn my music on (*London Grammar* – dead cool), look at my photos on the pin board, drink my tea, and lie surrounded by all the kind thoughts of my family and friends. Not a bad start to the day after all.

It's now 8.30 am and time for my big birthday treat. I dive into a bowl of Kellog's Crunchy Nut Cornflakes, which arrived in my canteen yesterday. Fantastic! We do get a daily issue of prison cereal, which has been pre-packed somewhere out in the Gobi Desert. This by the nature of the distance it has travelled, is always a distinct taste disappointment, so it's great when you can supplement it with some real breakfast stuff.

The excellent news is that I've been able to do a deal for a toaster for 1 oz of burn, from a gentleman who is leaving in a few weeks to new climes. When he goes we can complete the transaction, and I will be able to have weekend delights with my orange and lemon grapefruit marmalade, that I make in my kettle.

Feeling sufficiently alert and clear, I put on my own possession t-shirt and old shell suit 'esk, tracky bottoms, which I can now wear as I am an Enhanced prisoner. I only wear them at weekends, as a defiant gesture, rather than a fashion statement, if any of you were beginning to wonder. Trainers are the big fashion icons to impress with in here, for which I am saving hard (like yer trainers Bruv, how much?) My prison issue black plimsols or daps will have to do for now.

They open the trap door at 9.15 and I'm out (and dressed) like an Olympic athlete, sprinting down the landing and down the 6 flights of stairs in 10 seconds flat, to reach the cleaning store in 3$^{rd}$ place.

We are allowed a bucket and mop on a Saturday morning to clean up the cell. There are only 4 sets of equipment and a

45-minute window of opportunity, with 134 prisoners on the wing. I stand proudly on the podium with my cleaning apparatus, but have to listen to the Scottish anthem for the guy who came first.

By 10.00 am *Saturday Morning Kitchen* is on, and my cell is spick and span, bed made, everything all tidy, and I can sit with a second cup of tea whilst I torture myself watching all the things I can't eat and drink.

I fetch me newspaper at 10.30, which is the last weekend, that I will receive one. Marvelous Minister Mr Grayling, has ordained that newspapers and magazines now fall into the same category as books, and can't be sent in from outside. We can still buy them, but they have to be out of our prison earnings, and my 9.50 per week, won't stretch to such frivolity. The last thing the government wants is for prisoners to be able to read, write, and communicate with each other inside, or any other human beings on the outside, when they are released. He feels this is a big step in his cunning plans.

At 11.30, we go down, landing by landing, to pick up our brunch. I've ordered a bacon bap, and there is now a change in policy (as of this weekend), in that we can't have an egg or tinned tomato with it, which you get if you order the sausage and waffle. Although I am furious, I remain calm and return to my cell.

We get banged up at 12. I read my paper and then turn on the ladies Wimbledon final. We get let out at 3, for an hour in the yard, (which now contains the planters wot I planted), and have a vertigo enhancing circular stroll for 45 mins. The fresh air is as marvellous as ever. Costa Del Dartmoor does have good air, and if you want to develop insanity at the same time as clearing your lungs, it comes highly recommended. Most of the boys are discussing and betting on the likelihood of Rolf Harris running the Art Class sometime soon.

We get our high tea at 4.50 pm. Today I've ordered Lamb Madras with mushy peas), but I ditch the boiled potatoes for cous cous that I've made in the cell. The big splash is my birthday trifle which consists of a blueberry muffin, tinned fruit cocktail, tinned custard, and a tin of cream.

I wash it down with a special small carton of guava juice which have been introduced onto the canteen list for Ramadan.

Forgot to borrow a bloody can opener! Have you ever seen a celebrity chef charging round his kitchen, screaming profanities at his staff because he can't find the can opener.

Flip… the fruit cocktail and custard tins don't have ring pulls. The dream and planning is all over. I have a blueberry muffin with a dollop of carnation cream on top. There's something in the muffin which gives it a life of around 2.5 years and tastes a bit strange. It's alright though. No candle on top in case I set fire to my cell.

Anyway, banged up, and Argentina v Belgium on the telly. Who gives a shit? I turn the TV off and try a little yoga on me bed, but fall off with my right big toe in my left ear. So I put on a CD story book on the Borgias instead. In all, not a bad day.

# 6.  WE'VE GOT ISSUES

The magazine workshop gathered on Friday mornings to engage in discussions of various levels of meaningfulness about how to proceed with the writing, editing and production of the prison magazine *Tor Views*.

Dartmoor had had a magazine for over ten years. It had somehow managed to stay alive, stapled by hand, written by enthusiasts and distributed to the 600 or so men on the wings. The contents were random, ranging as they did from the Pagan chaplain writing about the celebration of the Winter Solstice to the most expensive jar of marmalade in the world.

As an 'accountable activity' a magazine workshop benefitted the Prison Service because it provided measurable hours of purposeful activity, helped to improve literacy and enabled departments to advertise their services around the prison (drug treatment programmes, charity initiatives, new courses and so on). As importantly it enabled prisoners to develop their writing from handwritten, misspelled, unpunctuated and in pencil on scrap paper to an edited form on a computer from where they could then see how best to present it on a lay-out. Thus, as writers, it prompted the necessity of engaging the reader as well as being part of a team striving to achieve the same thing.

Articles for the magazine were collected by the editorial team from their mates on the wings. No photographs could be taken, as cameras were not allowed, so images had to be made using clip art and Gimp, the free software that happened to be installed on the computers. We didn't have Photoshop, only Microsoft Publisher – an extremely old version about which everybody complained. There was no colour photocopying, so I printed the magazine covers on a Staples printer in Plymouth, bought them in in boxes, and we hand stapled them to the rest of the magazine. We argued about branding, fonts, proofing, contents and lay-out.

It was all quite punk. Well, I thought so. I had always been romantically involved with the history of print's relationship with poverty and dissidence and with the necessity of publishing to serve a purpose rather than flap about waiting to go into the bin.

The first issue, painfully collated in the spring of 2013, was printed on the prison photocopier with admin women coming in and asking if I was finished yet and was I using the prison paper and me bright red in the face and nearly dead of boredom watching the endless pages flap on top of each other.

Then, getting hotter and hotter and more and more embarrassed, I laid the pages out on the floor with the prison officers walking around me as they came in to collect their post. I was glad of the yoga because, once down there on the floor with the stapler and cardboard boxes, preoccupied, it was difficult and disorientating to come up again, from all fours. Then there was loud complaining from the editorial team about the standard of production.

'Why are the pages in the wrong order, Jess?'

'Why's my name spelled wrong?'

'Why did you change my article?'

'Security stitch us up?'

'I don't know and I don't care; I've just hoiked five boxes of the bastards through five locked gates across the prison courtyard in the rain and up twenty-five stairs.'

It was slightly easier when I bought staplers for the group and everyone collated and stapled, though not without dismantling the staplers to see how they worked and arguing with each other about how many biscuits had been eaten during the tea break and Colin launching endless debates about the Government.

In general, though, I was imbued with the same useful imbecility that makes mothers love their ugly children. I thought *Tor Views* was good on its own terms. The magazine was very well designed, professionally paginated, proof-read, formatted, and contained correctly informed and balanced articles that were of interest to and accessible to the 600 men on the wings whose concerns were unique to them and of no importance at all to anyone outside the prison gate.

The cover of the autumn issue bore a fine black and white illustration of Dracula by a biker turned tattoo artist, and a report on the Prison Council, where the issues raised had included whether prisoners would be allowed to have electronic cigarettes, to the filth of the waiting areas in Health Care, to the fact that clothes (always known as 'kit') were being distributed that did not fit because the large sizes had run out. This, as various members of the team pointed out, was not the only problem with kit. Boxers often arrived ripped and smelling of urine 'and worse'.

No prisoner has personal underwear – there was a kind of dreadful communal pile in the laundry from which the boxers were distributed willy nilly, in every sense of the phrase. We discussed the possibility of running an article entitled 'Pants – The Truth'.

Under 'Dartmoor Prison News', 'Pets Corner' described 'the possibility of guinea pigs and bees coming to the prison after the success of the battery chickens which, having been rescued, now run free range in the Resettlement Unit and are laying 40 eggs a day.' There was a pathetic picture of a newly arrived chicken – thin and featherless – and another of the same animal, restored to health, 'after ten months in D Cat conditions – fully rehabilitated and ready to resettle.'

One of my favourites was the story entitled 'Snow White: The Evil Within', where Snow White was not allowed to call herself 'White' but 'of European Origin' and where she was condemned as 'sizeist' for describing her friends as 'dwarves' and then arrested for being 'prejudiced to the vertically challenged'. She was forced to change their 'stereotype' names from 'Sneezy' to Allergically Sensitive Person and 'Dopey' to Person with Learning Needs. Happy and Doc were allowed to keep their names while police investigated whether Happy had 'substance misuse problems' and Doc's qualifications were legitimate. Collectively they were to be described as 'The Seven Shorter than Average but Still People in Their Own Rights'.

The Letters Page, entitled 'Have Your Say', featured a letter from a man who had stabbed his wife to death. It began, 'Dear Sir. I'm not one for moaning or threats but I would like to draw your attention to the fact that while I am currently serving a sentence at HMP Dartmoor my teeth have remained in Parkhurst prison.'

A report on a meeting of the Equality Action Team minuted the problems that were arising because clothes were being flushed down the loo, that there was a bad smell of damp on Arch Tor (A Wing) and there would be a delay in re-roofing F and G Wings, despite the fact that the rain came through.

Book reviews were led by a young man in, like many, because, 'she lied about her age.' He preferred *Crime and Punishment* to *The Idiot* but had found Chaucer very boring. He read a lot and wrote the reviews for the magazine – a section vibrant with enthusiastic eclecticism. Unfettered by any pressure to describe books that the publishers wished to promote, the criterion for inclusion was based entirely on an individual's taste and the wish to tell other prisoners about what he had read.

Autumn 2012 carried a review of Lewis Carroll's *Alice in Wonderland*.

This is a classic. We've all seen the film and this is it but on paper, trippy and mad, probably written by an acid-taking weed-smoking hippy but part of old British culture and of history and for that alone worth a read.

*Diary of a Young Girl* by Anne Frank was called, 'The best book I have ever read'. Terry Pratchett, Stephen King and his son Joe Hill were ever popular; a furious anarchist (in for decommissioning bomb release mechanisms at a weapons manufacturer in Sussex) was a fan of Will Self, while the late Iain M Banks received a full-page eulogy and was described as one of the 'great novelists of our time'.

Another wrote how Graham Greene had changed his life and was delighted when I told him that the author was said to have enjoyed taking drugs and having sex with most of the genders that were available to him at the time.

The enthusiasm was infectious and I re-read HG Wells on advice received from various reviewers. True crime was popular, as was the graphic novel whose characters were part of common parlance and whose validity was argued for in an article entitled, 'Graphic novels – are they just comics?'

'They are easy to read,' said the writer, 'even for those who are not confident readers, and the art work is amazing.'

Simple enough stuff, you might think, though of some importance when remembering that illiteracy was part of everyday reality. Many prisoners could not spell, punctuate, construct sentences or format work; what they did have, in many cases, was ideas, originality of perspective, and unique experiences which, in the end, are what the writer needs.

So in came the story about the seagull who was too depressed to fly and the story about the thoughts of the man walking up the steps to the guillotine. There was 'Tony the Giant Squid' and an article about what would happen if Davros, the leader of the Daleks, drove himself into the prison chapel.

There were many avenging gnomes and over-armed Viking mutants who were less the fault of Tolkein and more the fault of Peter Jackson *who has a lot to answer for*.

I discouraged those who thought they were going to earn a living from writing. 'You will have to get a job.

Writing is a pastime and a pleasure and a distraction; it is a craft and it is a lottery. Very, very few people actually make a living out of it and they are not necessarily the ones with talent.'

The summer issue of 2014 had made us all revolve on the carousels of our broken office chairs, so amused were we by our own jokes, but it incited all kinds of complaint, and was banned by Governor's Order. Of course being banned is a compliment, but it is also a bore. A terrifying diktat went up on the noticeboards, which read:

**NOTICE TO STAFF**
Business Plan Priority: Communication
26 July 2013

It has been brought to my attention that the last two copies of the Tor Views magazine have generated adverse comments and complaints from a number of staff and prisoners.

I have decided to withdraw the magazine from publication until I can be satisfied that all adequate censorship by a committee of staff and prisoners across all grades can be formed to ensure that no further articles can be considered to be inappropriate.

It is unfortunate that I have to take this action, as I believe that Tor Views is a publication that both staff and prisoners enjoy reading. A further notice to staff and prisoners will be published asking for volunteers to form a censorship committee for any future publication of Tor Views magazine however as stated until this committee is formed no further publications of Tor Views will take place.

The trouble, it seemed, had arrived from several sources. Reception, which the prisoners saw as a nasty little empire with too much power, had objected to an article impugning their efficiency and honesty and they had written A Letter of Complaint.

The 'Mormon Bishop' had arrived in a fluster because George Michael had appeared on the faith page in an article about, 'The Church of Jesus Christ of Latter Day Saints,' and he was a homosexual and they are not allowed, or don't exist, or something; anyway everyone got het up.

Someone who had never been a heroin addict complained about a joke made about the physical appearance of the queue to get methadone. Then, the final straw: the Prison Officers' Association complained. The union's motives remained mysterious but it didn't help that an elderly paedophile had described them as 'Nazis'.

As a result of all this the magazines were removed from the wings and hundreds of copies had to be secreted into the bottom drawer of a filing cabinet.

Prison officers, by the way, aren't Nazis; they're more *Porridge* than pogrom. The uniformed staff at Dartmoor were unusually nice, sometimes eccentric in a good, gold-toothed way, often extremely funny and all doing a badly paid dangerous job that would have made any normal human being feel murderous.

This view was not necessarily shared by prisoners, who endured a different relationship with the staff on the wings coloured by the nature of the prisoner (self-centred, needy, dishonest, paranoid, bored, impoverished, hungry, uninformed, ill-educated, self-harming, opinionated, scared, angry and, quite often, in physical pain) in a regime applied by uniforms whose job it was to control the petty incidents of everyday reality where the stakes could be very high (suicide and murder) and very dull ('Don't hit me, Rogers, I can't face the paperwork.')

We were more careful with the next issues. Autumn was a good excuse to celebrate Halloween, though I vetoed blood spatter on the cover. It was too near reality. There was a man on B Wing who had butchered the three small children he was baby-sitting and thrown them out of the window. Their mother returned home to find their bodies impaled on the railings in the street. The prisoner designing the page did not know this, but I did, and I thought of those children every time I saw the crimson motif.

The designer refused to let go; the splotches kept reappearing, proof after proof, there they were again, a little smaller, less splattery, but there. They looked good graphically so I gave up and they stayed. Dexter was going into his eighth series – splatter was the common parlance of forensic fiction. You always worry about the wrong things. Who could have seen the George Michael problem arriving? Nobody. Not even the Lord Himself with His alleged omniscience.

This time most of the jokes were aired in the air rather than committed to paper. MedZ wrote an article entitled 10 Reasons Why I like Hitler ('Number 6: His Smile'). The argument for this contrarian approach was that he didn't want to hate Hitler just because everybody else did. That is, he was saying that he distrusted received opinion and felt suffocated in a monoculture, a position with which it was fairly easy to agree, particularly as unthinking obedience had contributed to creating fascism in the first place.

'We can't run the Hitler article,' I said, and staple-gunned it to the Board of Honour alongside a picture of Peter Capaldi and a sign saying 'No Singing'.

Hitler, an undying figment of the collective unconscious, came up quite a lot. One man didn't turn to the magazine workshops for a couple of weeks because he was in the Segregation Unit following the discovery of *Mein Kampf* in his cell. He had told me that he was reading *Mein Kampf* and I had been rather impressed; it is, after all, the source of important information about the genesis of an idea. I hadn't put it down to a security issue, but Mr K's interests were obviously translated differently in the more volatile culture of the wing where philosophical dialogues were not the norm and serious worry about gang culture was.

We always had to be on the alert for gang culture – there was a written warning about it as you came into work: gang culture, drugs, radicalisation and mobile phones.

Post ban, the autumn issue was to be approved by a 'committee' made up of people like the LGBT (Lesbian, Gay, Bi-sexual, Transgender) rep, senior managers and a member of the Prison Officers' Association.

This time they asked for the removal of a picture of Fagin (offensive to Jews) and a picture of Morph, a clay television character, who had been moulded into a naked male model with the caption, 'like what you see?'

The back pages of the early issues of *Tor Views* featured the semi-naked bodies of various females. The prisoners on the wings were encouraged to draw their dream girls. It seemed like a good idea; a way to engage the reader and motivate creative interaction;

rather their pervy eyes were trained on the willing, able and mature body of Lady Gaga than the victims of their records –victims which, in the case of one man on B Wing, was a cow.

'Is that illegal then?'

'Depends if it's consensual innit.'

'Apparently they're in love. The cow's gonna visit him.'

'Fuck off.'

I remained in a state of post-feminist political confusion about whether I was colluding with the dodgy history of the Naked Muse or encouraging a healthy approach to those who had been nicked having sex in a wood with a 15-year-old, or child rape as it is also known, as if all 15-year-olds were also 10-year-olds.

Colluding or communing? It would have been easier to reject, or at least argue against, the culture of undress if the Dr Who assistant and her ilk did not get themselves endlessly photographed wearing their bosoms. And that was before you had even arrived at the unlikely termagants who inhabited the world of computer gaming.

I had worn my own bosoms on occasion, decades previously, and was nervous about turning into a po-faced Old Bat, but I did regularly point out to the group, when there was the inevitable discussion about the physique of the latest body on the televisual street corner, that if a woman was good at what she did she didn't need to take her clothes off; the semi-clothed actresses who were admired in men's magazines were not destined to enjoy a dignified and respected career trajectory. Cate Blanchett didn't have to take her clothes off; neither did Kate Winslet or Emilia Fox.

Less clothes signified less talent, I argued. But they hadn't heard of Cate Blanchett purely for that reason; no appearance in the magazines and newspapers that they read. The soap opera girls, they exhibited. Everyone knew about them. They were topics of interest; Lily Allen was not.

The team was banned from any kind of Internet access, which did not stop them ensuring that Kelly Brook and her bra appeared on every single screensaver so that when the eleven screensavers lit up all you saw was hundreds of grinning Kelly Brooks, everywhere you looked. Kelly and her bras, a disorientating circle of them, and I didn't know how to get rid of her. Or them.

It was my fault. I had brought the picture of Kelly in, not realising what they were all like. To my relief the screensaver Kellies were gradually replaced with Cartman ('You're all tree hugging hippies') an Angry Bird dressed as Slash, some nuns with guns and, yes, your actual legitimate goldfish.

The magazine was asked to remove the pictures of semi-naked women by the new 'censorship committee' that had been ordered by the governor to read it for matters of taste and security. I ascertained that this request came from a female member of the prison service, and though initially annoyed, I came to agree with her. The language on the wings was relentlessly abusive about women. Female prison officers and civilian staff (drug workers and so on) were vulnerable, and if they were young their lives were made impossible by the leering and commentary by what was, after all, large packs with dog instincts, many of whom were serving time for crimes against women.

The guidelines about what was suitable for exhibition were outlined in a comprehensive list known as a Policy Statement.

HMP Dartmoor will not tolerate the display of any material which is or is perceived to be offensive. In essence any material which is deemed to be offensive by **any** individual viewing it. The item or material displayed, presents as disrespectful and potentially denigrates either the subject matter or the individual viewing the subject matter.

This made it clear that 'offence' is in the eye of the beholder; you can be offensive without even trying and by mistake. This meant that 100 people could laugh themselves stupid at a joke in the magazine, but one letter would provide effective censorship because one person was offended. Thus the imposition of the culture of 'diversity' did as much to incite the bored and small-minded as it did to protect the sanctity of respect.

There were nearly 1,000 people in the community in this fog-ridden patch on the moor; different departments, different wings, different worlds. Why do people read magazines? To find out things they don't already know about the (usually niche) subjects that interest them, to know what is going on, to feel a part of something. All of these things are of some importance where the boredom is interminable behind the lock of a cell door and where isolation results in a pronounced need to be heard.

In 2014 the Ministry of Justice's ludicrous 'reforms' were beginning to receive widespread criticism from many different quarters. The prisoners' already low quality of life descended further thanks, by and large, to the petty and unworkable IEP (Incentives and Earned Privileges) scheme that had been introduced by Chris Grayling (Minister of Justice 2012–2015) and his unfunny minions.

Their effects were best described by a prisoner who wrote about them for *Tor Views*.

## Prison. Is it all Play stations?

I am what is known as an 'Enhanced' prisoner. This means that I have shown the prison that I am willing to fulfil my sentence plan. A sentence plan is the programme that all prisoners are all given when we enter prison – it is designed to help us address our ' offending behaviour' by attending programmes such as ' Substance Misuse', education classes (for example, maths lessons or computer skills) or regular employment. I work in the 'textiles' department, sewing prisoners' trousers, for which I currently earn £11.50 a week.

Prisoners who wish to become Enhanced must also show that they are willing to do something 'extra' such as help with a voluntary scheme. For instance, I am a Listener which means that I am trained by the Samaritans to be 'on call' when a prisoner is very distressed or anxious and needs somebody to talk to. Other Enhanced prisoners may be 'Insiders' – where they provide information to other prisoners, or they might be a member of the Prison Council, which is a forum where prisoners discuss issues with governors.

If I was to change my attitude and not be willing to complete my sentence plan and was rude to prison staff and fellow prisoners and not be willing to work, my Enhanced status would be taken away and I would be put down to a 'Standard' regime.

'Standard' prisoners earn around £8 a week, (depending on their job); they have no games consoles or DVD players and fewer hours for visits. Enhanced prisoners are allowed £25.50 per week personal money while those on 'Standard' are allowed £15.50. Standard level prisoners can apply for their Enhanced after being on Standard level for three months.

The other two levels are 'Basic' which is given to a prisoner as a form of punishment when there has been bad behaviour, such as fighting on the wings. A prisoner on basic has no television, less time for visits, and reduced 'canteen' privileges, so he might not be able to buy extra food such as biscuits.

Prisoners on 'Entry' level are those who are newly convicted and have probably just arrived from court. They are on this regime for the first 14 days of their sentence. They have no television.

This system is all called the Incentives and Earned Privileges Scheme (IEP) and has been in the prison system since 1995. The scheme has been designed to reduce violence and sustain a community that encourages rehabilitation.

The prison magazine ran various articles describing the idiotic aspects of the IEP scheme while the image of Mr Grayling's face was transferred onto a can of baked beans and accompanied by the caption 'Reports have often mentioned the remarkable similarity between Chris Grayling and a baked bean.'

This, apparently, was too much; senior management asked us to remove it.

The prison service was, to an extent, represented by the content of the magazine, and, although we carried a regular waiver about opinions, the magazine editorial could not laugh at the government because the magazine was seen to be a product of the prison service, and the prison service could not be seen to be laughing at the government. Hilarious though the government is.

Mr Grayling visited the prison momentarily and spoke to one of the brighter, younger, noticeably talented and more ambitious prisoners who informed him that, as a sex offender (at the age twenty-two of he had seduced a 14-year-old), he could not see that there was any possibility of employment.

The minister scuttled away, charmless, ignorant and unable to engage. The offender, who worked on the magazine team, had the ability to be a professional graphic designer, amongst other things. He had tried to tell a cabinet minister what all young prisoners knew, that a prison sentence may last four actual years, but it is also a life sentence. The cabinet minister was subsequently replaced in a reshuffle. He had served for three years before his poisoned chalice was handed to Michael Gove.

Mr L wrote quite a lot of porn and insisted it should be allowed in creative writing as a representative of free expression.

'I have read Henry Miller,' I said, 'amongst many similar and I understand the position that pornography holds in the literary canon. It is an important position, and one that has been traditionally on the vanguard of breaking boundaries. But. You are not Henry Miller and you are in a prison. Freedom of expression is limited by this environment. This community has its own rules around acceptable practice and it is nobody's job to argue for progressive literary ideas.'

'Well, it should be,' he said.

A part of me agreed with him and I wondered briefly if it was my job, but then dismissed the notion. I didn't really like porno writing anyway (with some exceptions) and wasn't willing to go into battle for it in a culture where a lot of the men were rapists.

The same man was also doggedly collecting limited edition figurines from an official Dr Who monthly magazine. He brought each one into the creative writing session when they arrived in the post, proud of the immaculately painted features of the Ood and various Doctors.

Dr Who was a common language and the magazine workshops were often devoted to long arguments about which of the villains was the most frightening, whether the Cybermen were basically human and what was inside Davros's skirt. Everyone had a personal favourite doctor depending on when they were born, though no one liked the one with blond curly hair.

There wasn't anything Mr L didn't know about Davros and he wrote a long and interesting history of the evolution of the evil Time Lord and a timeline configured to the creature's development and efforts to take over the world.

'He wouldn't be able to get into the chapel, Jess. No wheelchair ramp.'

Mr L had been labelled as 'a danger to female staff', and though unthreatening as a person, his nonsensical short stories were full of deviant fairy tales. I would have been more unnerved by his take on the Cinderella story if I had not seen Lindsay Kemp's gothic operetta in 1995 in which there had been sex and mutilation.

## Cinderella: mutilation, sex, more mutilation

Once upon a time there was a big house with two ugly sisters and an evil stepmother and a beautiful young girl by the name of Cinderella. She was treated pretty badly by her step-sisters and stepmother, having to do everything for them, but one day there was a party at the palace with a handsome prince hosting it. Cinderella wanted to go but her mutilated stepsisters and stepmother told her she is not going. On the day the party was starting the two ugly stepsisters left for the party whereas sexy Cinderella had to do chores but then Cinderella had a visit by a fairy godmother that set up nicely with glass slippers, beautiful red dress and posh jewellery.

Cinderella went by pumpkin coach and beautiful white horses. When she gets there she dances with the prince and he then takes her to his bedroom and fucks her like she has never been fucked before and then she looks at the clock it strikes twelve and she runs off and leaves her glass slipper behind and by the time she got back she was in rags again. By morning the prince searched high and low for the beautiful young girl but he could not find her. When the evil stepmother heard the prince was coming over she went to shorten her feet by mutilating them and being ready just like the ugly sisters but when the slipper didn't fit there was no one else until he spotted Cinderella and asked her to rest a foot on his leg to try the slipper and it was a perfect fit they lived happily ever after and had babies too. But her stepmother and stepsisters they had their heads chopped off by a steal [sic] guillotine.

The magazine had a page for poetry that contained subjects ranging from the Basingstoke Canal to the Perfect Marriage ('Suffer her tantrums, soothe all her ills, say she is slim, pay all the bills . . .') plus the occasional haiku about liquid Thorazine. It was difficult to know who to blame for the popularity of poetry and the writing of it. Not Oscar Wilde; I showed one prisoner the *Ballad of Reading Gaol* and he said, 'Oh yeah. I was in Reading, it's a shit-hole.'

Well-meaning art therapists and teachers of creative writing, immersed in the caring culture of arts therapy, saw poetry as an important expression of inner pain and an outlet for release. It was also an easy way for less literate and less confident learners to put words together without sentence construction.

'Write poetry,' I would say, 'if you like (God knows I couldn't stop them) but I can't pretend to know anything about it, so I can only read and comment, I can't help you improve it because I simply don't know the criterion by which it is judged.'

They didn't take any notice of my disinterest – quite rightly – and carried on writing it.

S was on B Wing. He was eighty something, serving time for a sexual assault committed when he was twenty-seven. His victim had brought charges more than forty years after the incident. He said it was about money; the victim was now suing for compensation. 'My lawyer said I would get a suspended sentence, but then the Jimmy Savile thing broke . . .'

Citing Sir John Betjeman as a favourite, S wrote poetry and had compiled an anthology of over 100 poems during and about the course of his sentence. They reflected a literary education that had made the writer aware of the poetic use of a format that endlessly describes the seasons and nature – floating clouds, fruits of the autumn, eventide suns, gentle mists and placid lakes. The usual. But in amongst rhymes about shining sun beams there were the acutely felt observations of a man wrenched from home, in love with his partner, (to whom he proposed over the public telephone on the wing) and deserted by some but not all of his friends.

Imbued with an artist's acute awareness of time, colour and personality, his anthology reflected the minutiae of prison life and the personalities therein.

There was Mr F, whose only dream was to move in to a 'super-enhanced' cell; prison officers who sang whilst working, one with a 'doubtful bass; another with a voice that could 'start a race.' The ironing board is 'free today for those who wish to press', while inmate W was dropped on his head as a baby and a prisoner from Cirencester went to the chapel in order to ogle the lay preacher's tits.

Sid didn't go off the wing, but stood around in a space he had made with a group of other old men. He chatted through the slow day with N, also an historical sex offender, who had a triangular body support frame and was teaching himself Greek, which he wrote out in a red exercise book.

Poetry had been a part of Dartmoor prisoners' lives since the days that Frank 'the Mad Axeman' Mitchell lumbered about the wings. Frank Mitchell was not a rocket scientist but he managed to escape in 1966 with the help of the Kray Brothers, for whom he occasionally worked. The Firm picked him up in a Rover, drove him to a council flat in east London, and then murdered him.

It was quite easy for men wearing gold jewellery to spring Frank because he had long been allowed to join the group that worked on the quarry on the moor outside the prison. History says that Frank was quite lazy and, in fact, regularly left the work party to go to the local pub. It is said that he once walked into Tavistock (twelve miles away) in order to buy a budgerigar.

There was the inevitable nationwide hue and cry; roadblocks were built; helicopters were despatched; questions were asked, in particular, why a man as dangerous as Mitchell had been allowed to go outside the prison and provide a danger to the public.

The answer to this relies on some knowledge of how an insulated prison community protects itself and configures to its own lore, rather than the real law whose relationship with operational reality is sometimes impractical to the point of being both useless and dangerous.

Mitchell was a man who liked to show off his strength – he was allowed out of the prison and onto the moor because he was huge and afflicted with what today might be described as 'learning difficulties'. The man was more manageable outside than lumbering about on the landings inside with an inclination to violence and nothing to do except show his strength, which was considerable. Legend has it that he once lifted up a Triumph Vitesse police car with two officers in it.

Perhaps the last word belongs to the chaplain of the time who, having discovered Mitchell reading poetry in his cell, wrote, 'The man has a fund of fearlessness and courage which could in other circumstances have made him a very useful citizen.'

Fifty years later these words still resonate with any civilian who has worked with prisoners; the killer, the junkie and the fraudster write verse in longhand in pencil and in Biro, unpunctuated and misspelt and in capital letters. Men who have raped children and hacked their wives to bits write poems on scrap paper about the colours on the wings of a dragonfly.

## 7. I'LL TAKE THE HIGH ROAD

Two weeks after the death of Alexander Cusworth he was no longer a topic of conversation.

Colin expressed loud disapproval over the fact that Cusworth's cell had been tidied, cleaned and repainted in time for the visit from the victim's foster parents.

'I know *my* mums would think what the fuck, his room would never have looked like that.'

Colin didn't see his mums much, being as he had been in care and then in prison pretty much since his stepfather had tried to kill her. She didn't visit him in Dartmoor, neither did anyone.

So Cusworth's body lay as evidence in a morgue and his alleged murderer lay in a cell in Exeter prison. Jokes were beginning to circulate around the work-shops and wings.

'Have you tried to get a job in the kitchen? Apparently it's murder.'

Subjects had moved on to Christmas, which was long and boring, and the imminent smoking ban, which everybody was dreading.

December tended to arrive with warnings of the dangers of drinking the prison-made hooch. A notice said:

The festive period is upon us once again. Historically hooch is brewed in greater quantities by prisoners in the lead up to and over the Christmas period. Quantities have already been found in various places around the prison. Hooch is detrimental to the good order and discipline of the establishment and endangers the health and safety of staff, prisoners and visitors. Those prisoners found to be under the influence of hooch are more likely to argue become aggressive and violent due to the fact that the alcohol acts as a disinhibitor.

All sorts of odd ingredients form part of this highly dangerous brew which, if consumed, can cause serious health problems eg irreversible damage to the brain, mental confusion and disorientation, blindness and alcoholic poisoning which can lead to complete organ failure resulting in death.

All staff need to extra vigilant and mindful of the collecting and storing of items used in the brewing process. These may include: excess bread, excess fruit, bottles of water, bin bags, plastic bottles (e.g. washing up liquid and cleaning bottles).

Hooch is made in toilets, under beds, and locker spaces. Containers are left in bin liners near to sources of heat such as pipes and tumble driers.

Prisoners generally agreed that hooch was a disgusting fermentation process resulting in a stinking brown liquid that everybody said tasted 'rank' but 'did the trick'. It was often made of Marmite (for the yeast) sugar (stolen, hoarded or traded) and the fruits that were part of the daily ration of food apportioned to each man and then traded, especially the oranges. Receptacles were plastic containers stolen from rubbish bins, which meant that staff had to jump up and down on every plastic milk bottle and stab it with a pen in order to conform to security guidelines and prevent the detritus being taken advantage of by the kind of people whose skill sets did very well in Chicago in the 1920s.

Effective puncturing of the potential hooch bottles was difficult to achieve. It is very difficult to make a hole in a plastic milk bottle in an environment where all pointy and metal implements are locked in a 'shadow cabinet' with felt-tip pen marks denoting their position and only accessible to the person with a key, clearance and correct pay grade.

A lad on D Wing was not alone in his opinion that alcohol's effect on a personality was much worse than that of illegal opiates. He had tried both and had this to say:

Before we go into just how much grief this evil liquid can cause you and those around you I will say that as well as almost killing my ass on numerous occasions it has caused me to serve over twice as long in prison over the seven years I was an alcoholic than the heroin did in 17 years. The biggest sentence I done when I was on the gear was eight months. Since I been on the juice the shortest sentence I got was 14 months. If a heroin addict goes on a burglary he'll break in quietly when no one's home. And even then he'll scarper at the faintest sound; us piss artists will come through your front door like Conan the Destroyer while you're sat down watching *Family Fortunes*; everything is done bigger badder and more reckless than when you're on the gear. The heroin addict just wants a quick raise for his next score done as quickly and discretely as possible whereas there's no reasoning with the alchi; he's feeling invincible and no-one's stopping him because he's got a knife, an axe or a sawn off...

A man with a beard and a walking stick limped into the prison twice a week in order to 'spread the message' of

Alcoholics Anonymous. He seemed to be a determined and dogged person, with his AA materials contained in a battered suitcase, willing to brave all weathers in order to hold his 12 Step meetings. It's a long way from the car park to the gate lodge in the dark and on the ice for a man on a stick.

There was a slight kerfuffle when he first arrived, as Alcoholics Anonymous prides itself on 'anonymity' being one of its essential principles. This condition is impossible to maintain in a prison where the name of any man leaving his cell in the evening has to be recorded. Furthermore his name may also be announced over the wing Tannoy, and he will certainly be observed by the others on his landing.

'Where's 'e goin' then?'

'AA innit.'

'They get biscuits?'

No, was the answer to this; they were there to receive the 'message of the fellowship', not eat biscuits.

The Association of Chief Police Officers (amongst many others) has pointed out that, 'Nearly fifty per cent of all violent crimes is alcohol related. Offenders are thought to be under the influence of alcohol in nearly half of all incidents of domestic abuse and alcohol plays a part in 25–33 per cent of known child abuse cases.'

Extrapolated, this would suggest that of the 600 men incarcerated in HMP Dartmoor, 300 might find it useful to address the amount of time they had spent in the pub.

Alcoholics Anonymous prides itself on growth through 'attraction' rather than promotion but God is not an attractive brand. Nobody liked the 'God' side of

AA, though He is mentioned only once or twice in 12 Step literature before turning into the Higher Power, which is an entity described by personalised definition. The AA literature also points out that atheists (as likely to be alcoholic as anyone else, after all) have enjoyed a good track record in this realm.

'What do you think of the Twelve Steps then, Miss?'

'I think it's a good thing for people to do when they first get out of prison. The steps are helpful as ideas to help you address problems and the meetings are free, pretty much. There are people in there who might be helpful. You get a cup of tea and a biscuit. It's worth a try.'

'What about the God stuff then? It's Bible-bashers innit?

Sinking heart

'It's not really about God – more about learning techniques to help yourself stay off . . . '

'They got them meetings on A Wing, but they're on gym nights. I go to the gym . . . and he sits on his own in that room, 'im with the AA. I feel sorry for 'im.'

Meanwhile, on the drugs front, Spice was on the wings, and notices went up warning everyone that they could die from it.

Spice, also known as green crack, is supposed to be a psychoactive designer drug created by spraying natural herbs with synthetic chemicals in order to produce effects similar to that of smoking cannabis. Its manufacture, unregulated and haphazard, meant that its safety was far from guaranteed. Prisoners on it were disorientated and clumsy; they did not know who they were or where they were; they were seen shouting at invisible demons and falling over. They could be seen in the G Wing yard at the weekends, semi-naked, kneeling, literally shrieking for their mother. Nobody seemed to have a nice time on Spice; it wasn't a good advertisement for itself, except as the crudest form of escape.

'It's difficult for anyone in uniform to tell who is off their heads and there are no tests,' said one prisoner. 'These people have no idea what they are doing while under the influence...'

Nobody actually did die, not of Spice, anyway, but there was a close call one night when several prisoners collapsed and had to be ferried to hospital in a flashing motorcade of ambulances.

At 5.30 p.m. a twenty-two-year-old was found unconscious on G5, followed by the discovery of another prisoner on the same landing drifting in and out consciousness and being violently sick, then another, also semi conscious. As several ambulances arrived from Plymouth along with teams of paramedics, a prisoner told one of the officers, 'You'll have a load more tonight as there's some really bad stuff on the wing.'

Drugs tended to be hurled over the wall by a civilian whose arrangements had been made through the use of a smuggled mobile phone. The mood-altering substances changed according to availability and demand –one month there might be a lot of heroin on a wing, another month people were swallowing their Subutex and regurgitating it to be taken again in an activity known as spitback.

Drugs were hidden inside various receptacles – dead pigeons, dead hedgehogs, deodorant bottles, fruit. In one case an abandoned (live) baby owl came under some suspicion, but was later cleared and received a complimentary profile in the local newspaper. In another a woman was seen on farm grounds next to G wing communicating with a prisoner of G4 landing. When questioned she stated she wanted to see her partner on Christmas day.

Drugs, contained in what were described as 'suspect packages', were once sent through the post and were invigilated by useful Spaniels until budget cuts rendered the Spaniels (and their Labrador colleagues) redundant, meaning that the hours worked by the dog handlers were reduced to a minimum and certainly not enough to inspect the daily pile of post.

Dealers and addicts, far from stupid, saw such problems as opportunities; as personalities dealers would go far in management, as *The Wire* so correctly illuminated. The dealers always did very well on the 'Business Enterprise' course in Education, which was no surprise to the Plymouth self-made billionaire, Chris Dawson, who was quoted as saying before a planned visit to the prison:

'Top criminals often have the best entrepreneurial minds. If I can help them turn their mind to business and help them stay out of trouble then that's great.'

One Saturday the Oscar 1 (Duty Governor) had to investigate when a remote control helicopter landed in one of the yards, innocently as it turned out, a child's toy, but you never knew. Drones had been seen attempting to drop drugs into other prisons.

Dartmoor was no worse than anywhere else; the only prison rumoured to be free of drugs was HMP Wayland (a Cat C prison in Norfolk) and that was because there were Highland Cattle in the surrounding fields and the dealers were too frightened to walk past them. I mentioned this once to a governor and he said that, as a strategy, Highland Cattle probably wouldn't work in London. Anyway it wasn't true as subsequent reports revealed that Wayland was as vulnerable to smuggling as any other prison.

Governors would hold regular 'amnesties' and advise prisoners to hand in the bad stuff (including any contaminated needles) as it might kill them. Another Governor's Order might warn prisoners of the punitive (rather than health) consequences of taking drugs that, after the Spice incident, included being placed on closed visits, being placed on a basic regime, twenty-eight days of cellular confinement, loss of pay, and twenty-eight days with no canteen, spends or private cash.

Consequences, however, are not a feature of the addict's thought process. If they were there wouldn't be addicts. They wouldn't be Mike, on steroids, in fights, stabbed in the eye and blinded; Micky, twenty-five, Hepatitis C, on drugs since the age of nine when he saw his drug addict father's legs purposely crushed by a jeep driven by his creditors. Micky was trying to reduce his 'script' despite being diagnosed with testicular cancer. He was about to get out. He wanted to be 'there' for his dad.

M was on G Wing; in conversation during a creative writing class he said that he thought Dartmoor was a 'nice little nick' and the 'food was amazing'. A long-term 'substance misuser' (as it is termed in the polite parlance of the professional practitioner), M wanted to stay off. He had children. He didn't want to come back to prison. So he did P-ASRO (Prisoners Addressing Substance Related Offending) and wrote about his experience for the prison magazine:

When I first started P-ASRO I did not want to be there. It took me a week to come to realise that I needed to do P-ASRO to address my drug problem – but being on P-ASRO has made me realise that there are loads of people in this world with drug problems and that I am not the only one. I have met some good lads on the course and we have all got a sad story. We all come together to help support each other on and off the course and I have made some good friends. I have overcome my demons with the help of the P-ASRO staff and the people I met on the course. If I am feeling low and want to have a use up I know that I can go and talk to one of the lads that I have met on the course and they can do the same and come and talk to me. P-ASRO has given me the skills to believe in myself and that, with the right thinking, I can overcome my cravings. No matter how bad life seems to be or what it throws at me I don't have to turn to drugs or other substances because life is never as bad as it seems. The staff are all amazing and friendly. I would say to anyone who is thinking about addressing their drug problem P-ASRO is the way forward.

**MedZ, dishonourably discharged from the army, in and out of jail, on and off crack, was a self-harmer, had mental health issues and 'problems with women', according to people who knew him. He was also a gifted cartoonist and a perceptive and original writer. If he had 'problems' with me he managed to keep them hidden.**

**Following reports about Russell Brand's appearance in the House of Commons to argue for radical reforms in drug policy, I asked MedZ to write an article for the prison magazine answering the question 'Is Russell Brand a Plonker?' He produced the following answer:**

## MedZ says

You might not know it but Russell Brand used to use heroin. Ten years ago his agent caught him smoking heroin in the loo. He booked straight into rehab and the rest is history. Recently you might have seen clips of him in the news with his new campaign. Basically he is saying that the Government should decriminalise drugs and in the next breath he is saying stop giving Methadone to heroin addicts in favour of 'abstinence'.

Now I like heroin and the idea of abstinence sends a chill down my spine just as the words 'decriminalise' sends one down David Cameron's. I think, in reality, every addict's dream (including mine) is to be able to purchase drugs – but hang on a minute! Drugs are already legal – and the dealer? Well. That's our doctor.

Here at Dartmoor they are doing a cracking trade, as they are in every other prison, and in every GPs surgery in the UK.

Russell says, 'We might as well let people carry on taking drugs if they are going to be on Methadone, obviously it is painful to abstain but at least it is hope-based.'

Russell seems to be working some of his 12 Step philosophy in helping others but also, in my eyes, not accepting his powerlessness over others. He is trying to change a massive problem, but I suppose someone has to start from somewhere so why not him?

Abstinence based recovery is much cheaper than keeping people on a Meth script and would reduce crime, says Russell. In April he even spoke to the government Home Affairs committee about their drugs policy. He told MP Keith Vaz that politicians don't know what they are doing. They don't understand the reality of the way people use drugs.

Maybe we should ask Russell if he fancies being an MP instead of a comedian. He's already half way there.

**Colin was not alone in wanting to know more about IDTS. Even the long termers didn't know what the**

letters stood for. Frank was, 'Smack 'eads, fuck 'em,' while Nick thought it was sinister that the Head of Security was also the Head of Substance Misuse. But nobody actually knew what IDTS was or what it was supposed to be, just that it was the queue for Methadone and Colin wanted to be on it. But then he always wanted to be on something and, over the years, had been on pretty much everything, as he so clearly described in one of the articles he wrote during the Creative Writing classes.

**Cannabis**: When I was young I used to smoke weed a lot. When I was 13–14 the aim of every day was to get stoned walking down the road with bottles to our mouths as it was all bongs back then. But I got PARA quick on weed and stoned quick for that matter. I was always a lightweight. Bongs used to kill me off after a few, like someone had tied a brick to my lungs and let it hang. My mate used to be able to do bong after bong; he was like a machine blowing fat smoke rings across the room. That always used to secretly impress me even if he did end up shagging the Thai bird I was chatting up. If you like questions then you'll love getting stoned, my mate Dave first observed this and it's so true because your perception of time does change and slow down. It's like *Mastermind* on speed, questioning everything, a quick fire round lasting hours, but I was always too paranoid to think of anything but my paranoia. My paranoia is bad when I'm stoned.

If I was walking down the road by myself I used to think cars were gonna stop and kidnap me.

I actually once spent what felt like hours in some garden hiding as a result but in reality it was probably about 20 minutes. In houses I used to think I was being spied on through keyholes and windows. I remember at Jasmin's vividly zoning out at this keyhole seeing this boy running around then stopping with his eye right up to the keyhole and this happened repeatedly. It scared the shit out of me and this is on weed so you can see why I was never gonna do acid. I should have stopped smoking weed sooner, in fact I only passed up weed in preference to being sober for the first time about 2 years ago. I smoked weed because when your monged it is nice and when I was younger I would have done anything not to be sober, anything was better than me, my head and my life – even severe paranoia.

**Speed**: Speed for me is decent but never my first choice of drug. Speed's better than nothing (I don't dislike whizzing off my face) but speed's more scatty, erratic and hyper whereas pills is pure love and I love that. I always associated speed with speed fiend mums that I knew. It's used for dieting by some girls. I do like speed and I've done my fair share of it.

It's good for beginners line by line or dab by dab. If someone offered me a gramme now I'd snort it but my heart lies with ecstasy.

**Ecstasy:** I love E's and I deny that to no one. I always have been a fan, show me one person who doesn't like being wrapped in love! I was introduced to E's and looked after during my first few times by a couple older girls, they were like 15 and 16 or something, but that was still older than me. They started me on half then I progressed from there.

They looked after me, kept me safe and made sure I was alright which is what I needed as coming up can be panicky for first timers. They broke me in gently and I appreciated that. Raving on E's is amazing like completely at one with yourself, with others, with the music. I love it. E's make trance what it is and there's no surprise that I also love trance music.

Standing in a rave arms out spread like a crucifix eyes shut, music blaring…bliss. I was in some drum and bass club with this tramp I met and we got chatting to a couple of girls. One of them went and the other one, a brunette in a short skirt, took us back to hers. She lived with some other people in this house. We all bedded down for the night and me and this girl was doing things on the sofa and the tramp was in the chair but then he starts throwing a strop because he was jealous. He should have been grateful for the roof!

He said he was going and that I just used him for the drink like guilt-tripping me; he wanted me to go with him and like a mug I went. But the girl slammed the door in front of me, she was like, you ain't going nowhere, I was, like bloody hell you're committed, then I left and I actually ran after this tramp. I can't believe I passed her up, to say she was giving it to me on a plate would be an understatement – she was force feeding me, and I left, what a mug!

My thing on E's is squeezing. My bottles of water get mangled. I love laying with girls especially when their buzzing as well just squeezing the shit out of each other but if she's not buzzing girls get pissed off all I hear is you're hurting my hand, babe, then I apologise through a locked jaw. They know I don't mean no harm. I can quite happily do E's by myself and have done on quite a few occasions. I will always end up on missions but I'm quite happy to buzz by myself listening to the tunes ringing everyone up seeing what's going on. Anywhere and anything is at least good on E's you will always see the positive on E's no matter what the situation.

I remember being in a phone box with a girl trying to ring people to sort things and we must have been in there 20 minutes and I loved every minute of it. I was thinking ain't these walls good keeping out the wind, it's cosy in here and we've got the phone if we need anything. That's the way E's make me, in reality I was in a phone box for 20 minutes but you live and buzz on the feeling and where the feelings consistent it's all good like everything so that's how I love everything on E's.

When I first started doing E's me and L had a bit of a thing me, her and B was in B's bed and things was leading up to sex. I had saucer eyes anyway but the thought of this widened them. It's something I very much would have welcomed. B's fit as well but she was 23 – a older more established member of the group if not the most established member.

I did look up to her she was the cool, sexy older girl she was like 16 and I was 13 or so – not quite a cougar – but at 13 one year is long so possibly out of my reach. L was more like me, she liked me and I liked her, but that night at B's where (it has to be said) she was leading, she was like we can't have sex because we might have a heart attack and even though it was only my 8th or 9th ever pill I would have been a willing participant, but it never happened probably rightly, as poor B was right next to us. It was only a double bed as well. It would of basically been a threesome (except B was not and would not of been involved) but we was packed in like sardines all of us stretching out, rushing…loved it.

On pills I smoke but I smoke non stop fag after fag, fags are gone like 20 decks in hours, splashing out and chain smoking, roll ups last longer but rolling up outside when it's windy and your eyes are flickering and your hands are shaking is not the easiest of tasks but it is cheaper and you can always ask someone to roll it up for you.

With pills where everything's good, bad things look good however it's dressed. I met this girl outside A+E, she was 30 and I was 16, she was fucked, she was a junkie who had shit herself. We got chatting and I ended up going back to hers, she give me a couple blues and went and had a wash. She lived in a dirty bedsit somewhere fuck knows what I was doing but we ended up having sex and she jumped on top. She was alright looking all things considered, a skinny brunette with a small cup size, but she had shit herself! What was I thinking? I made my escape the next morning and never saw her again…madness.

I was seeing a girl in Walton for a while. I used to turn up at her house unannounced at any given hour, fucked, and climb through her window, but I had to be careful because her dad was a big bald headed geezer and he didn't like me at the best of times so the last thing I wanted was for him to catch me in bed with his daughter (for the record dads don't tend to like me I don't know why must have one of them faces). She was cool though, her and D they was proper, good looking girls. Fuck knows how I knew them I've never actually lived in Walton so it can't be that, probably college or mates of mates or something.

We was all very similar and we'd all meet up somewhere or go Slough or Kingston or wherever go across to Leatherhead or Reigate to meet people or mission it down to Brighton or Bluewater or wherever just to get out of the area get up to mischief, chat and do things, anything to spice up the monotony of the roads...days out really.

N and D was cool but they were naughty. I never used to see them that often but shit always happened when I did. A security guard tried grabbing D up once in a shop, N hit him and I shoved him across the room and we all ran away laughing our heads off. Another time we was in Bluewater, D got nicked for shoplifting and left me and N stranded, but we had D's N.I number so we went and got a crisis loan in D's name, went to the bank, blagged a statement using D's N.I number and got a Giro cashable at the local Post Office.

It's clear to see I'm very fond of Ecstasy. I believe it actually heals the soul. I love it.

**Alcohol:** Alcohol is a bit of a nightmare for me. It's basically the reason why I'm in prison; alcohol in moderation and in the right frame of mind is very good, safe and in some cases healthy, but for some it's a jail term waiting to happen. Drunken nights out are drunken nights out. We've all seen it and done it so I won't go over old ground. Nowadays since my imprisonment I don't drink so much maybe on Christmas and birthdays but not that often really. I've been pissed in prison and I just get happy and relaxed. Alcohol doesn't affect me in the same way that it used to and that's because I'm not the same person. I've grown up, my teenage issues have been made insignificant they don't mean anything to me and that just comes with age.

I'm far more balanced in my head. I actually am who I am now instead of trying to be someone I'm not…better late than never I suppose. I was in a right situation at one point. I was transferring to Erlestoke to do the 12 Steps. The night before I done 2 ml of Subbie (off the block) and that morning my mate D had me downing cups and cups of hooch, kick, everything! On the bus I was swaying and when I got there they put me on the 12 Step unit but I said to them I don't need to do this shit course. I was like do I look like a fucking junkie? They weren't too convinced, I could barely stand up pissed out of my head and still half Subbied up from the night.

I've turned up at 12 Steps, a junkie rehab programme, off my tits claiming I don't need to do it, how funny, they must of thought yeah mate whatever you say. I still don't think I need to do it. I admit I do the odd bit of drugs but I don't act reckless or dangerous I just chill out and do what I'm doing. Anyone who thinks I'm spending potentially the next three years in jail drug free is very much mistaken. As if I'm gonna do that. Are they mad?

**Cocaine**: Charlie's a funny one for me because being the pauper that I am I can't afford 40, 50 quid a pop for a night out and that's a gram! I can quite happily get through two or three grams of speed and that would cost 20, 30 quid and better than that I could get 5 pills for a tenner and be buzzing all night. Me and my mate Dan had a phase on it but it never really floated my boat.

**Prescription Meds**: Valiums like diazepam are nice they have an opiate type effect without actually being an opiate. They're dangerous though if you over do it. People on drink are like oh I can't remember a thing the problem with Vallies is if you do too many you seriously can't remember a thing, it's just blank, days get wiped from your life and in that time anything can happen, you'll have a day out on Sunday and wake up somewhere Tuesday morning clueless anything could of happened and you'd have no idea.

**Zopiclone (Zoppies)** are sleepers. They're alright but you need three to buzz off it. I usually do three in the morning. The tinny taste is not ideal but then that's just an excuse to get the coffees on.

**Anti Convulsants**: Anti Convulsants dumb down the electrical currents in the brain therefore relaxing you, there alright like gabbies are half decent, you need a minimum of 1200mg but ideally between 1800 and 2400 to buzz off it.

**Opiates:** I love opiates but I've only been using them since I came to adult prison. Gear (heroin) is nice there's no denying that especially if it's a proper Joey and it only cost a top up (which has already been paid) the tapers, the foil it's a bit of a ritual. The thing with gear is it's 10 pound a pop and you're only gonna get one hit off it and it will leave you wanting more and self control can crumble. Three for £25 is the one, all on the foil I was doing that and you do feel nausea and I have thrown up before but it doesn't matter at the time, you think oh well time for another coffee and roll up and you start cleaning again smoking gear makes me CLEAN! But despite this on a budget like mine you can't afford it and half the time it's cut to fuck anyway, for me the whole package is Subbie, and Trammies a close second.

**Subutex** (Buprenorphine) like Methadone is a heroin substitute used in heroin detox. I've used both Methadone and Subutex recreationally and Subbies is the one for me. It's clean it's safe and it's cheap; for the price of a half ounce of burn you can get fucked all content, cosy and ruby. It's nice, like heroin, it numbs the physical and emotional side to a person so you feel nice and relaxed (talk about silver linings ha ha mate your life's fucked but here's something to make you feel ok about it how funny!) personally I love it. It's my little treat every now and then.

Believe it or not I'm not a scumbag, criminal minded, addict. I am at best a drug enthusiast. I don't mean any real harm I'm just living life and, for the record, I happen to be a half decent boy.

IDTS, as it turned out, stood for the Integrated Drug Treatment System and was one of the multitudinous and occlusive arrangements with which the addict engaged on his mystifying journey through the system of prison-based 'substance misuse treatments'. Described in Prison Service Instruction 45 as, 'A joint service of the Department of Health, Ministry of Justice, and National Offender Management Service', the aim of the IDTS was to 'increase the volume and quality of substance misuse treatment available to prisoners'.

Dartmoor, a training prison, was expected to 'manage' prisoners who, 'had already been stabilised in a local prison'. Prisoners who have committed 'sub-stance related crimes' are not expected to be abstinent but to be engaged in an inexpensive clinically regulated regime which will allow them to take on, for instance, education courses or offending behaviour programmes. Thus they go on IDTS which is, basically, a queue in a space between the Library and Diversity where the edentate, the thin, and the hopeless receive a plastic tumbler of Methadone from a woman in a blue uniform.

'Methadone doesn't treat addicts,' said Colin, having the last word, as was his custom. 'It keeps them quiet. Methadone is cheaper than drug-related crime – it is cost-effective, but it's not treatment. It's containment. Maintaining people on Methadone means that the Government has admitted that the problem cannot be 'cured'. They don't know how to treat it and it costs too much to try and find out, so addicts are allowed drugs, but not on their terms.'

# 8. COLIN

My first sight of Colin was as a lanky manifestation lying on a desk in the Education Department. He bore a resemblance to Ian Curtis and announced that he was on anti-psychotics. He did not further his popularity in the Education Department by threatening to set fire to various teachers; they took that kind of thing very seriously. The security department had listed him as an 'arsonist'.

'I went on the roof at Guy's Marsh, didn't I?' he mentioned.

'Why?'

'I dunno. When they asked me what I wanted I said a cigarette.'

He had spent most of his twenty-four years in care and in prison. He moaned like hell about everything and was incredibly annoying in that way that adolescent boys are annoying – not listening, going on, pushing for fun, testing boundaries, going on. But he had, as it turned out, a high IQ, which might well have been the source of some of his problems – he asked endless questions, had imagination and a critical faculty and was easily bored. He was also affected, unexpectedly, by an ability to write which bordered on an actual talent and about which he was completely unaware.

His 'issues' were infinite in their number and his suffering had been immense but there was a gentle soul, flashes of self-awareness and an interesting raw intelligence. If his launch into life had been different he would have sailed through higher education and likely qualified to work with animals as was his 'dream'. But he had never had a chance. His first memory, at the age of about five, was of his drunk stepfather beating up his mother. Colin and his younger sister were in his bedroom when they heard his mother screaming. They thought he was killing her.

His mother was about to stab her husband to death with a kitchen knife when Colin's sister walked into the kitchen. The stepfather turned on the little girl, and the mother ran into the bathroom with the telephone and rang the police. They arrived as the man was smashing the bathroom door off its hinges. There was blood all over the walls. Colin helped clean it off with a towel knowing that it would happen again. But it was years before the man went to prison and Colin was taken into care.

The state saved his life really, that is what he thought anyway; the stepdad from hell would have killed him, or he would have killed himself, sick and tired of the unrelenting abuse. He remained grateful for that. Being saved. His mother and sister had to stay where they were. He acted out and got out.

Colin was on an IPP for GBH (Indeterminate Public Protection order for Grievous Bodily Harm) and had no release date. He had beaten a man up and kicked him in the head. It was the kick that got him the IPP, 'when they were handing them out like sweets'.

On paper he looked like a violent recidivist, trouble-maker and nutter. In real life he was very easy to like, and he was liked. There was a lot of rolling-eyed bloody 'ell 'ere he comes, and everyone nearly died laughing when he became the 'Thinking Skills Orderly' but when Colin's mother got breast cancer Alex, often driven mad by him, delivered the recycled newspaper to his cell so he could do the crosswords he liked doing. No puzzle was beyond him. No book too dull for him. All subjects were of interest.

He came, vaguely, from Guildford; expressed a desire to live in Gatwick Airport, had been moved around Sussex and Surrey by Social Services, done foster homes, group homes, family homes, B+Bs, hostels, and hotels.

Colin knew, as he knew so much, that there are no government rules on how to give just the right amount of affection and emotional input. He said he was happy to let drugs give him the warm feelings of acceptance, contentment, love and affection. He was rarely silent, and if he was it was usually because he was too miserable to speak. Or he was coming down from Subutex.

In Colin's view care and drugs came hand in hand but it was the girls who fared worse, as drugs led them into prostitution and abusive relationships. He saw it all the time. Once, when he was fifteen, he was in a foster home in East Surrey and a twelve-year-old girl there could not be left alone with adults because she had been sexualised as a little girl and always offered herself to men.

Then there was another girl, older, between thirteen and fourteen. Her face had been slashed repeatedly with a knife. She had self-harmed and self-mutilated.

She had done it because she was being abused in the family home and didn't want it to happen anymore so she made herself 'ugly' in an attempt to put off her abuser and stop the repeated abuses against her.

Colin was consumed with his own life and couldn't cope with anybody else – he couldn't get involved when they unravelled in front of him; he was unravelling himself.

He hated foster homes, but he didn't mind being in care so much; he didn't feel loved in the care homes but he liked his mates and he liked taking the piss out of the system. He made friends easily because, chronically displaced, he sought relationships wherever he could find them, because he had always been moved on and he knew there wouldn't be much time. The mates came in and out of his life because they tended to turn up in the same prisons, on the same wings.

Sometimes he committed crimes for financial gain, but mostly to get things out of his system. He had done quite a few burglaries ('them detached houses have got pound signs all over them'). His octopus arm could fit through small gaps. He would bend metal coat hangers, pull the handles from the inside and get in that way, until his arms got too big.

He enjoyed shoplifting. Sometimes he would go in, put a crème egg in one of the girls' pockets, then, when they got out, he would pull an egg from his own pockets and say, 'Guess what we've got in common?'

He usually went for cosmetics, but it was an effort getting rid of them. The junkies were good at it, though they were always a bit obvious with their big coats in summer and their big bags when they were patently penniless. He saw one being chased by staff, darting out of Tesco with two legs of lamb. Meat was always popular. It was how Rick on F Wing had got done; when he was stopped with a leg of lamb under his coat he told the police that he was defrosting it for his mother.

Colin sought revenge on his 'stepdad from hell' and stole the man's credit card. He ran up £3,000 debts buying Lambretta coats, FCUK tops, jewellery, and Tina's Christmas presents. He bought mobile phones left, right and centre and dished them out to his mates. It was great knowing that he was hurting the stepdad, even if it was only a fraction of the amount that the man had hurt him. The free stuff was good as well.

The sweetest thing was pawning the stepdad's wedding ring. He got next to nothing for it but that didn't matter; the act was very satisfying. Occasionally they would rob people at cash points which, looking back, was something he regretted.

So Colin, chronically displaced, came from nowhere, and had no base. And there were thousands like him, lolloping about on wings all over the country, all with similar case histories, all abandoned and damaged and violent.

'From 0–13 I was abused and hated, from 13–21 I was in care, from 16–18 I went to prison three times and from the age of 18 to now I have been in prison solidly! From 16–18 I got three prison sentences for theft from a person, arson and GBH. I kinda saw prison as an escape, a place to run to, exiting the real world completely.'

Men always think they are going to be raped and beaten up when they go to prison for the first time and Colin was the same, playing out the horror stories of soap dropping and Borstal Boy scenarios. He knew a bit because his mates had already started to go in; one was in Feltham on remand.

The first thing he noticed on his first night in HMYOI Huntercombe was the banging; people banged on their doors like jungle drums – when there was a goal, when someone they knew was on *Crimewatch*, or at the end of *EastEnders*. Colin learned to read the banging and, if the football was boring, he would change the channel until the banging signified that there was a goal, or replay, or something.

'When I got to Huntercombe, or "Huntz", as the boys called it, I was put on Howard, the induction unit. It didn't really dawn on me until they slammed that door shut for the first time, bang, game's over, that's when it sunk in for me. A bedroom with a toilet and sink, no door handles, graffiti on the walls, flaking paint and barred-up windows.

'The first night was a rough night's sleep, shouting, screaming and banging all night, people bullying out the window and I was there smoking roll-ups not knowing a soul. It's a hard situation to be in like that's when you feel lonely and like what the fuck is going on? What is my next move? But that's really just for your first ever night in prison.

'Prison is a completely different world and it does take some getting used to but we are as people adaptable. The first night is the hardest and it gets easier from there. I was the first within my social circle to be sentenced to prison although I was quickly followed.'

He returned to Huntz to serve another sentence when he was seventeen. By this time he was self-harming, quite seriously, using anything, a comb and a plastic knife in one incident, so the blood was all lumpy and stringy and he could pull it out. He was on Valium and blues.

'I was in more situations this time round, situations I didn't want to be in. Some boy from Luton –some short little boy thought he was all that being flash in front of his mates –he called me up and he was like, 'Give me your canteen sheet so I can fill out what I want.' I was like, 'Nah, that ain't happening,' and he was like, 'Alright we'll see innit, watch what I do to you.' And that was my welcome to Huntercombe. I should have said, 'Fucking hell, give me a minute. I've just got through the fucking door,' but that's how it is in YOs. It's persistent, consistent and ruthless.

'There were so many west London boys. I was surrounded by them, most from the gang RSG (Robbery Squad Generals). I was in between two of them, actually, and I passed weed and that through the pipes from one to another and passed burns and that. We sort of kept each other sweet. I am about as far from the street as you can get, like a gangster I ain't, but it just happened that I was between two of them and it was in everyone's benefit especially as we were next door to keep the peace and harmony. They'd sort me out when it was good for them to, so it was good for me.

'Staff got me to do a pilot CBT course (Cognitive Behavioural Therapy) which was OK. I didn't really know what was going on. It was only one-to-ones and sometimes with another boy just answering questions and pointing out the face that looks angry and sad and that 'Why do you think he is sad?' It's basic stuff but hmm I do wonder why I was asked, they must have thought I needed it. Anyway I got out of there alive and in surprisingly good spirits.'

Colin walked out of Huntercombe at the age of eighteen having served five months of a twelve-month sentence. His social worker picked him up. He was nice, but dull, so the journey to Horsham seemed to take ages. Social services had got him a flat and were paying the rent on it. It was a block for young professionals. Colin knew he was young, but wasn't sure about the professional bit. He had never worked a day in his life, as he was the first to point out. 'Professional isn't the word I would of used but it was nice of people to be so optimistic.'

So he had somewhere to live, and in a short time various girlfriends and street mates were taking drugs in the flat and scaring the neighbours.

Days were spent in Tesco nicking Disaronno or going to Brighton to score pills. Nights were spent smashed on E. He was chucked out and, over the next four months, lived in Bed and Breakfasts, in hostels full of pissheads, and on sofas. The girlfriends worked in One Stop; their mums and dads were junkies in and out of prison. The male friends were on probation, on remand, and on drugs.

Then, inevitably, he missed a meeting with his case worker, which meant that he was recalled to prison. This time he went to HMYOI Aylesbury.

Aylesbury was very different to Huntercombe, even if he did meet up with some old mates. It was young offenders serving life sentences, so you can imagine what they are like; 20-year-olds in for murder. It was different to any nick Colin had been to before. The atmosphere was menacing. When he had been in Huntercombe and Reading it was boys trying to be men; in Aylesbury they were hardcore. And they were sex offenders. Rapists.

The sex offenders weren't bullied but they were never allowed to forget they were filth. Colin and his mate would wind them up by putting 1p fruit salad sweets into the locks of their cell doors, which meant they were locked in until 'Works' (the prison buildings and maintenance department) came to sort it out. This could take a long time, getting Works over; they were always busy somewhere else. Sweets in locks were not a priority. Meanwhile Colin and his mates would open the observation flap of the hapless prisoner's door and say, 'No assoc tonight, mate.' The VP would respond, 'Yes there is.' Then Colin and his mate would say, 'No there ain't, not for you,' then slam the flap, laughing their heads off.

There was one fat boy, in for rape, who would say to Colin, 'Wank off for me and get your knob out . . .' Colin would pretend that he would do stuff for burn then, when the fat boy went and got it, he would tell him to fuck off. He got the hump but Colin didn't care.

There were always alarms sounding off and things happening. A teacher got stabbed in the head by a Turkish boy. The Turkish boy was doing twenty-four years for a double murder. He broke up the mirror in his cell then stabbed the teacher in the head. He made friends with Colin down the block. He loved Michael Jackson. Then there was an oddball who raped and killed a ninety-year-old while she slept and another guy who had raped his disabled sister and was discovered when their baby's blood was tested.

Colin got himself transferred from wing to wing; he hated being in one place for long. He was always running. Sometimes he wondered if he was running from himself. Prison was a great place to escape to; you could turn your back on reality and some of his best friends were in prison.

He didn't think he was a criminal or even particularly criminal-minded. He didn't scan for opportunities to commit crime; he acted when opportunities presented themselves. He had hurt people, but he didn't boast about it on the wing, not like some of the others, the young 'uns making themselves known. Yeah. I 'ad a table thrown at me, and all that.

Colin saw himself as well mannered. He confronted with words rather than violence. He thought people looked stupid when they fought. He had stolen cars and started fires but with no intention to hurt; actually, with not much intention to do anything, as he never considered consequences; all he wanted to do was feel better.

Then, in his early twenties, he started to have psychotic episodes. 'Epping', he called it, short for episodes. Everything would become very distorted. He would find himself linked to people he had never met, as if they were soul sisters and brothers from a family linked via the next dimension. But he also believed that people were out to get him, being controlled to do him harm. One time he thought people were being programmed by the prison service – chipped- and given orders to execute him. Another time there were demons possessing people to harm him. It was very surreal. He used to see human shadows on the wall. One used to stand there pointing at him and the other (who was nicer) used to play the maracas, which made him laugh. When he was in the shower he used to hear a girl calling his name from the drain.

'People assume they know about psychosis and psychotic disorders but they don't really. They don't know that in the space of three to six months a person can go from being normal to consumed by his own distortion of reality.'

Faces came out of the wall, like in the Doors song. They were always bald and they vibrated differently; he had to tap the walls to get rid of them. They were more of a nuisance than scary. The television was a nightmare because it always seemed as though the people on it were talking to you personally and sending you messages. One minute you're watching *EastEnders* and the next minute the telly's been smashed and you've got a knife in case someone kills you. Everything got very distorted.

He knew when it was starting; there would be a slight obsession over theories or ideas and distorted sounds. If the kettle clicked off he would read it as a significant sign telling him something, dick or prick, or something like that.

When he was 'epping' things would hit him like revelations or epiphanies and he'd be like yeah it all makes sense now. He went through a phase of turning cups upside down because he could hear laughing coming from them –nothing persecutory, just annoying.

He would get fixed on definitions, like free will, for example, and how people didn't understand the meanings their conscious mind had been led to believe. They're not actually choosing to do what they are doing. People turned into shells and were puppets trying to get close to him.

He could hear animals as well like dogs barking and lapping up water, ducks quacking, cows mooing, birds squawking. There was a farm in his head. It was very draining and it could go on for months.

'We as epping people are persecuted and oppressed for interpreting life the way we do and that is wrong.'

Still. It wasn't great that he became consumed by the thought of killing people who had wronged him. On the whole, though, it was OK as long as the stress levels were low and he was sleeping. The brain had to be calm. He believed that the epps were stress related. He really resented the fact that he had never got the help he knew he needed.

'Write your autobiography,' I said firmly. 'Write it all down. You have a voice and a story and I would not say this if I didn't mean it.' I did mean it. As one person he symbolised the spawn of the urban hell created by the 'new' Labour Government when (amongst the three thousand laws they passed) the Indeterminate Sentence for Public Protection was introduced.

Here was the real product of Whitehall; a breathing example of the actual effect of law and a reminder of how the body that the prisoners described as 'that lot in Westminster' affected the life of an individual. Though, as Colin himself was quick to assert, it wasn't entirely The Government's fault. What could they do?

Few people in the outside world knew him or where he was. He felt the slow dissolution of his relationships, not knowing what to say to his friends, losing contact. He didn't get visits, not in Dartmoor, miles from anywhere and too expensive to get to. And even when mates did come he hadn't seen them for so long it was difficult to know how to make conversation.

Colin had no boundaries. He was like an octopus – limbs everywhere, legs sprawling on desks, arms around other prisoners, driven by a bottomless need for physical affection, doubtless propelled by the fact that he had never had any; in care they don't touch you, you see, no way. It is all polite and formal because nobody wants to be called a nonce. The bacon factor he called it. So Colin was always touching everyone up, stroking, hugging, bearing down. The guys hated it, but in classes we laughed about it.

'Colin! They don't want you over there,' I would say. 'And they certainly don't want you to kiss them!'

'You always ruin the fun.'

'Is there any chance of you doing any work today or are you just going to hang around being useless?'

'I'm not in the mood. I'm going to Braille.'

'You don't do anything there either.'

I often wondered why I loved him.

I, as a civilian support worker, and female, had to work out how to be kind, helpful, effective, and authoritative while retaining distance and integrity. Most of the time I flew on the fuel of unfathomable instinct, displaced feelings of maternity, perhaps, having had no children, with no regrets, but there was the possibility that some animal part of me, some indefinable nurturing energy, had been displaced and, like trapped water, was seeking its own channels to the sea.

I did feel for the men I had got to know when I allowed myself to dwell on the reality of their existence, because prison is hell. It is a warped environment where everyone is walking very slowly uphill with the wind against them in a constant psychic struggle to obtain or maintain the slightest advantage.

Occasionally I would encounter a young woman and her small children walking up the hill towards the prison visits hall, to meet Daddy. Children and mothers, innocent and chatty, looking forward to their grey excuse for interaction, an hour sat opposite each other; the children, if lucky, not old enough to know where they were, their present made strange by Daddy's 'hotel', their futures predicted by endless depressing statistics about the effects on families fractured.

My deepest responses were triggered by men who had natural talents that had been suffocated by circumstance, and were unable to thrive in a loveless environment where jobs and education were aimed at the lowest levels of ability and achievement. And they tended to graduate towards me, possibly because there was nowhere else for them to go.

In October 2014 Colin was transferred to a D Cat (open) prison. It had been a long time coming, so he was quite surprised when it happened. They sent him a letter, then there was a two-month wait, then he was told the night before. This was prison policy. Men were only told of their transfer the day before. It prevented them making plans for escape. He was seen to have lessened his risk to the public so he went off in the van to a prison in Wales. He left behind a cardboard box full of papers. They were mostly letters from girls, decorated with hearts, expressing love and concern for his welfare. The girls were important to him; he would mope if they didn't write, as they were his only relationships, developed through the mail, like Jane Austen characters.

'Can you get rid of this, Jess?'

'How?'

'I don't care. Burn 'em or something.'

'Are you sure?'

'Yeah.'

He was the only prisoner who cried in front of me.

# 9. ART what is it good for?

In 2013 the education department's new employer, Weston College, decided to 'deliver' an NCFE Level 1 in Art as part of its shiny new curriculum. The NCFE Level 1 Certificate was a 'qualification' awarded by an organisation (NCFE) based in Newcastle Upon Tyne. Its website admitted that the acronym didn't mean anything, the acronym had turned in to a proper noun with capital letters, like GCSE. It was difficult to know what would happen to the person who announced to an employer that they had an 'NCFE' – presumably it wouldn't be LOL. Or GFY.

This art course lasted three weeks and I was employed to help deliver it as a 'substitute' teacher because I owned an obscure certificate (Preparing to Teach in the Adult Learning Sector or PTTLS) for which I had paid £300 to do the relevant course in a college in Plymouth. It was impossible to fail this course so it was £300 quite well spent.

The art room was next to my classroom and all part of the Suite with No Name. It was decorated with posters about Cezanne and Dali, an old kiln locked up with a padlock, two easels, some shelves with dirty old spineless books and a locked metal cupboard in which poster paints and plastic palettes were kept. There were various sizes, colours and thicknesses of paper in a cabinet whose lock had long ago been jemmied. A notice said, 'Only One Prisoner In This Cupboard.'

The aged resources consisted of limited supplies of acrylic paint, limited supplies of paper, one or two pencils, some old and dirty palettes of water colour, three pencil sharpeners (depending on who had stolen one) five rubbers (depending on who had stolen one) about thirty aged paintbrushes, flared and hairy, no glue, no scissors, and, for some inexplicable reason, a vast amount of those crayons that work with water.

The internal dynamics of the Suite with No Name were erratic. Members of staff came and went with no explanation. One minute they were there, the next they weren't and *nobody talked about it*. It started with the original art teacher, a sixty-something lady who was revered by the prisoners. No warning, no reason, no art and no art teacher. Another tutor, employed to deliver a life skills course (preparing CVs, interview techniques and so on) also vanished over night. Will he be coming back? I finally asked. No was the response with no explanation.

It was unnerving and dispiriting and symbolised the eternal murk of the prison state. Inexplicably, at the same time, a neighbouring classroom was painted lilac but remained empty except for one new table, one broken office chair and a box throwing up discarded pamphlets about health.

It would be very easy to argue that I was completely unqualified to teach art to anyone. My experience with its practice, although long-term, has been entirely personal and concerned with ideas more than technique; my knowledge of media is based on the use of it in a laughably amateur manner and does not include much interest in drawing, therefore I have little of the technical ability that is usually associated with draughtsmanship. I can talk bollocks about theory if necessary, but that wasn't going to be of much use.

I didn't let patent ineptitude get in the way, as I had not let being damn near tone deaf prevent me from running the music group on Tuesday nights. As the music group did not mind that I neither sang nor played an instrument, so the men who came to achieve an NCFE art qualification did not know that my sole experience of public exhibition had been to knit a naked dolly in the shape of Anna Wintour and hang her in a cupboard at the Port Eliot festival.

Luckily the art course was very basic and the learners didn't know anything about anything. They couldn't name the primary colours and certainly did not know what colours they made when mixed. Nobody had ever visited an art gallery. Some had never experienced a book, and didn't really know how to handle them beyond, 'Was this expensive then, Miss?' before finding the one and only picture that portrayed Pamela Anderson.

'That's by David LaChapelle.'

'She's alright for her forties innit, Miss?'

'Forty! She's at least sixty.'

'Nah . . .'

The debate about Pamela Anderson's age could go on for some time.

The NCFE art course provided a total of sixty hours of tuition or GLH (Guided Learning Hours) as they were also known. Prisoners had to make a 'portfolio', not of their art, particularly, but of sheaths of forms that had to be filled in by both the teacher and themselves. The magnitude of this paperwork was such that the writing, reviewing, assessing and personal planning could not be realistically achieved within the time allocated to do so – an opinion shared by teachers with years of experience.

Each prisoner was given a Weston College Offender Learning Services-branded Individual Learning Plan that announced their name, User Learner Number, a box entitled 'LEF: Yellow to MIS', the course title, the unit, the results of their initial assessments, their long-term objectives, their short-term goals, their unit targets with agreed and planned end dates, their personal targets, their equality and diversity support if required, their SMART targets (Specific, Measurable, Achievable, Realistic and Time Bound) and their own review of their targets, to which they were asked to answer the following questions: Was the target set at an appropriate level? Was the Unit achievable in the time given? Was your achievement recorded appropriately?

The tutor then filled in a box with his or her own 'review' and whether the certificate had been distributed to the learner. Certificates, in fact, took months to be distributed to anyone and, in the event that the so-called award signed by OFQAL did turn up with the man's name spelled right, he had probably transferred to another jail or was out on licence and had long been forgotten and, even if someone had recorded his address, he wasn't necessarily at it and, anyway, could be of no fixed abode or living in Poland, to where he had been deported. So the certificate itself, though much wanted by the learners on the course, for their probation officer if nothing else, was delayed by the eternal assessments that had to occur on top of the paperwork involved in the internal and external moderation process.

This was just the beginning. The learner was also expected to write a daily 'work diary' and fill in an NCFE activity sheet where twenty or so questions were asked on the three units that comprised the course. At the front of his folder there was a 'matrix' or column of boxes where he was asked to show the 'moderators' evidence of the learning he had achieved. There was also a candidate statement attesting to veracity, an end of course form and a feedback questionnaire.

The substitute teacher (£17 an hour before tax) was supposed to fill in candidate observation forms every day, for every individual, recording what work had been achieved and how that work evidenced the units provided. There was also a 'cognitive or learning weaknesses screening test referral form', where a checklist of 'potential weaknesses might produce a cluster', making it necessary for a 'Lucid LADS screening test' which would provide the basis for intervention.

Interventions included, 'mind mapping, ESOL, heavily lined paper, overlays, amplification and bridging'. The specific learning difficulties process came with a flow chart – thirteen boxes and arrows – where number seventeen was a 'provision map to be reviewed weekly.'

It took some time to come round to the sense of this. Why not let the artists express themselves and become better at art? Drawing and writing tend to be separate efficiencies unless you are lucky enough to actually be Mervyn Peake. The prisoners who had genuine visual ability were the exact same prisoners with the lowest literacy skills.

On the other hand many of the prisoners were so illiterate that it became possible to accept the logic of building writing into the course. One does have to write after all; literacy does make you employable; the ability to draw a horse does not.

On the first day I found the 'art students' talking amongst themselves.

Reiss: I was in anuvver prison, yeah, smoking spliff in my cell. They couldn't find it, but they could smell it. 'E was like I'll get you soon. I squirted Fairy Liquid in his eye, then I was on the block then back on the same wing with the same officer! Is Parky down in Seg ven?

Gwynn: Yeah. Mr A reckons 'e'll do five years for that – we were stood in ve dinner queue – officer said something about parole – 'is eyes started rollin' in his head and everyone scattered – 'e's a big lad Parky – I seen 'im hit a thirteen-stone bloke *up* a flight of stairs.

Reiss: There's no guvs around, Bro. The amount of shit that goes down . . . they're out to prove it at the end of the day innit . . . we're the product, that's all we are, we keep feeding them by coming back to jail . . . the prison's mad, Bro, there's no money . . . it's hard to find a mop on the wing . . . I'm going to start voting for UKIP . . . This government fing, it's a money fing, this country is not in a position to let other people into the country.

Gwynn: My oldest daughter is mixed race but it's like if you put 320 people on a boat made for 300 it'll sink, won't it?

Reiss: Personally I think Margaret Thatcher done alright for this country . . . this is what I don't understand yeah, I'm a Muslim yeah, but why are there suicide bombers when committing suicide is one of the worst fings . . . if I had to fight Syria I would for my fellow Muslims. I don't give a shit.

Gwynn: I lost my faif . . .

Reiss: I go to Friday meetings.

Gwynn: You Sunni?

Reiss: Yeah – my dad's Estonian innit. I was in Estonia for a couple of months. Polish people they come over 'ere for a year and they work hard, Man, we're like a lazy country . . . my Dad's got three businesses in Estonia, he lives like a king over there, Man.

Gwynn showed Reiss his forearm on which there is a tattoo from top to bottom.

'She stabbed me believe it or not with a comb yeah. It ain't affected my strength but it just don't look nice.'

The chaplain arrived to deliver a letter to Reiss.

'When's the imam coming back, Miss?'

'I don't know,' the chaplain said. 'He's on extended compassionate leave.'

She gave Reiss a letter which told him that 'security' had refused his request to lead the Muslim prayers on Friday in the absence of the imam. He was not surprised by this decision, and neither was anyone else.

The first week saw two troublemakers sent back to the wing for reasons that were slightly difficult to fathom but apparently involved the word 'titties'. The troublemakers refused to remain in exile and G Wing sent them back to the classroom. One of them, a mixed race lad in his mid-twenties, didn't want to be in education because he had a job as a, 'wing cleaner innit,' he only, 'come because my friend told me to.' He has 'done art' in other prisons.

The problem was that if he was sent back to his cell he would receive an IEP – a piece of paper where his behaviour was counted against him and where he risked losing his television if relegated to a 'basic' regime.

I made several telephone calls to various people to try to clarify the matter. It turned out he was a wing cleaner but also had permission to do education if he wanted to. His sympathetic landing officer said he could come back if he caused disruption in the classroom but, 'It should not be up to them to choose where they go and what they do.'

A bored person from G Wing was a liability in a classroom. I requested a November (a prison officer who is a roving escort) to accompany the bad-tempered student back to the wing.

The November failed to arrive. There weren't ever very many Novembers available. If there was one on duty he was usually occupied with the endless stream of prisoners travelling to and from Healthcare.

The only other way of getting rid of the resentful outlaw was to either wait for him to become violent so that the General Alarm could be called, or attempt to engage him in the activity that he so expressly did not wish to do.

There seemed to be no way of getting him back to the wing, and, after graciously accepting apologies for the mistake that had been made to his perceived disadvantage, he settled down to copy a picture of a motorbike while boasting about his various exploits in a loud voice which, as it turned out, included supplying Class A drugs and rioting in Gloucester. He spent the rest of the session trying to flirt.

'You're posh aren't you, Miss? Do you hold your sherry glass likes this?'

'I wouldn't dream of holding a sherry glass, like that, or in any other way.'

At the end of the afternoon he said, 'Thank you, I had a nice day,' as if he was leaving a children's party.

The most surprising learners showed the most ability. The youth on anti-psychotics really could draw but could not for the life of him write anything down. Introduced to the idea of collage, he started off with a black plastic rubbish bag in order to make a nightclub scene.

'I've stuck my pictures up in me cell, Miss.'

'What with?'

They weren't allowed Sellotape (possible garotte) or Blu-Tack (possibility for making imprints of keys).

'Toothpaste.'

'Well, take them down, you need them for your portfolio – you have to be able to show you've done some work or you won't get the certificate. And please don't rip anything up. Art is a process; everything is going towards something, so there is no such thing as rubbish, only stages. Crap doesn't matter. And anyway you have to show the process in your work books.'

'Is there a certificate for this, Miss?'

'Yeah. We get £2 for the certificate innit?'

'It is called the NCFE Level 1 Certificate in Creative Craft.'

'So, no use for getting a job then.'

'Do we get paid if we can't come 'cos of CARATs?'

' It's not CARATs any more.'

'SMS innit.'

'I done that TSP.'

'She's fit that Miss in there. I'd do 'er.'

'You'd do anyone . . .'

The sharing of ideas was an activity that had to be 'tracked' and 'evidence referenced' in Unit 01 assessment criteria 1.5. Teachers were told that, 'Ofsted are very keen on discussion at the moment.' This meant that both learner and tutor had to note down what was discussed and how ideas were presented, which in turn meant that the spontaneity with which such things occur was ignored and that discussions and ideas were curtailed and clipped before they could become either interesting or helpful, because they had to be recorded in endless boxes.

'Do you think *collage* is a pretentious word?' I asked the group as we looked at a picture made out of tissue paper and magazines by a fierce man in tinted shades who addressed me as 'Guv'.

'What does pretentious mean?' was the answer.

'It means up itself. *Collage* is also known as *decoupage* . . .'

'That's worse.'

The discussion demanded by Ofsted would then descend into chaos as a frightful old cove (in for supplying teenage boys with alcohol and molesting them when they passed out) would start a side argument with whoever was sitting next to him; a lifer would scream that Tracy Emin was rubbish and the general conversation would become a long debate about the authenticity of the attributes displayed by the various Essex women seen on one of the few television channels the prisoners had access to.

I would take a fizzy headache pill, breathe in and out to remind myself I was still alive, and try to restore order by introducing subjects that I knew interested them. Like how and why Van Gogh had cut his own ear off and that he had made no money at all when he was alive and was now trading for millions.

'How's that happen then, Miss?'

Difficult question, the one about why a very good artist is not seen as such during the time of his life and work. How does one explain that to anyone, let alone a person who has been excluded from school at fourteen because he fired a staple gun at the art teacher and whose visual literacy is entirely expressed in the hundreds of pounds worth of tattoo he has spent weeks having distributed down the side of his body.

'Van Gogh was before his time,' I said lamely. 'People weren't ready for his work so they didn't buy it.'

'He drank a lot of that absent stuff didn't he?' said the one who was always late because he was doing a 'Substance Misuse' programme. 'That's why he was so colourful.'

'He probably did drink quite a lot. But so do a lot of people and they don't paint pictures like that.'

The general consensus was that it was probably a good idea for Van Gogh to cut his ear off from a publicity point of view, but I explained that it wasn't really. This extreme measure had not done his career any good and he had been in a lot pain.

'He was depressed and had mental health issues.'

This they understood.

A quiet man drew a forest in great detail then asked for a list of statistics pertaining to stateside deaths by capital punishment. Asked if this information had anything to do with his art project no adequate answer was provided. The request for this particular resource was undermined by the discovery that he was in prison for hoarding a stun gun and potassium cyanide and had a history of harassment. On searching his rooms police had found, 'a GPS tracking device, a claw hammer and literature about abduction and murder.'

No, then, was the sensible answer to the request for information about the use of the electric chair in the United States of America, but the delivery of it was difficult to provide without talking to him about his offence, which wasn't easy to do.

If worried about the behaviour of a prisoner, staff were advised to provide information to the security department on a form called an 'S.I.R'.

'Where are the SIR forms?'

'There aren't any. It's all Mercury now.'

Mercury was part of a computerised system to which I did not have access at that point. The possibility of declaring concern about the disturbed hoarder for the good of the security of the prison and its personnel seemed remote. He kept asking:

'Did you get that list, Miss?'

'Didn't have time, sorry – shall I come and look at your drawings, hmm, very good, well done.'

The men liked being told about the properties of the various HBs and they liked sitting down quietly and calmly and copying quite boring pictures of cottages out of reference books with unconfusing titles like 'How to Draw Anything'.

The majority were naturally inclined to make images that were graphic, measured and patterned. Some of them were brilliant at perspective and many liked Mondrian when they were shown pictures of his work. I wondered how confused they actually were and whether the drawings were a way of sorting things out.

The most inventive and capable, talented, if you will, were often also the most withdrawn.

Jack was a quiet man in his twenties, watery-eyed, cynical, clever, on a short sentence, he could make anything out of anything and did so. He was brilliant. We both loved making objects out of interesting detritus. I had had a long admiration for Kurt Schwitters; he had been encouraged by his mum who went to car boot sales. I affirmed his talent; he didn't know he had any.

Most prisoners had chronically low self-esteem. They knew they were the lowest of the low; they were in a prison, which was literally the last one before you fell into the sea, Dartmoor–the final dustbin. This mindset, while understandable, did little to help them address the enormous challenges that would present themselves both in everyday life on the wings and in arming themselves with the braggadocio needed to obtain a job. So if art was there to help this then so be it; art has many purposes.

'This is my last session,' Jack said one day. 'I'm going to work in the concrete workshop.'

'Ah,' I said. 'Do you know what they do there?'

'Sort of . . .'

'They make stone statues and paint them with glossy paint,' I explained. 'They are designed to go into the garden. They make tiny cottages and Alsatians and cupids and iguanas with the name of your house on them. The workshop was known as Gnomes when I first came. I laughed out loud about it until I worked briefly behind the till in the museum and saw how popular they were. They sell *really well* all those little men and penguins.'

'Well,' he said, 'I dunno. I've only got three months left. My mate is there and he says it's OK.'

In some ways prison was where real art happened, where art was to do with soul and instinct and psyche and all the other indefinable mysteries of the human depths, rather than the ability to conform to the complex protocols of art world politics and economy.

Prison art defied judgement because it could not conform (it did not know how to), and it didn't know what the rules were let alone who was writing them. Its purpose as part of the process of change, whilst complex and usually unfathomable, was nevertheless occasionally apparent. Art, or any creative activity, even at its basic crayoning and glitter glue levels, allows reflection and it allows self-expression, both of which could provide answers to the questions that all prisoners were supposed to ask themselves. Who am I? What were my mistakes? How can I avoid making them again?

The lifer, in for killing his ex-boyfriend, didn't boast about this murder exactly, but he did make high-pitched allusions to it. He said it had been all about a pair of shoes, then caught my eye to see if I would laugh. I implemented my usual practice of pretending not to hear, and then becoming inappropriately hysterical once I was out of the gates. Victims were not a laughing matter, even if one was a long-term fan of Joe Orton and understood the dark humour of gay sensibility.

The lifer produced quick results with a wide range of media and used his sketchbook as a diary to work out a complex range of personal thoughts about his life and about his offence.

The latter had been committed in 1998, and the offender, like many of the men in for murder, was one of the least frightening members of the population.

He was keen and interested and therefore a pleasure to teach. Notes were written, in private, in his cell, about what the work in his sketchbook meant and how the images had been created.

*'Pastel is quite a nice medium to work with . . .'*

*'The shape of the car is fine but the colour is wrong . . .'*

*'I have chosen to remind myself to look at the First World War and how it changed art . . .'*

*'Not too happy with this. I used watercolour pencil but it's all gone wrong.'*

*'You could say that I'm feeling a bit lost at the moment.'*

*'Sory is such a small word, so why did I spell it wrong? Maybe I'm trying to say that even when we say sorry it means nothing. All I've done is leave one letter out and it has left this word meaning nothing. Maybe I am getting fed up of saying the word and not being believed or heard.'*

Murderers (lifers) in C Cat tend to have committed one extremely violent offence, having reacted badly in the throes of jealousy, fear, drugs and drink – usually all four. They tend not to have committed any crime before, they often have records of mental health issues, and they do not cause trouble on the wings because they are not criminally inclined in the sense of the words where they apply to the person who is impulsively violent, self-centred and dishonest. They have taken a human life, sometimes by accident (during a fight), sometimes with intent, and they are put away to pay for this.

The lifers in Dartmoor had been in prison a long time, paying for what they did, but it could be argued they were less of a risk to the public than the repeat offenders, in for endlessly fighting and stealing and drinking. You lose it once, you lose the lot –that was the tragedy of many of the murderers.

Before William Tolcher killed Alex Cusworth in the kitchen I had always thought of the murderers in Dartmoor as being OK. The murderers were always polite and up for a long conversation. I had helped one with his tapestry and another with finding a computer to work on his dissertation. They didn't like it in Dartmoor much because it was not a 'lifer' prison. Theirs was a different experience to the rest of the prison population. It required a different mindset and a different set of amenities; distance learning, for instance, was very important to a lifer.

I had assumed that you could be alone with a murderer, in general, but you wouldn't be alone with anyone from G Wing, or some of the less stable sex offenders or the men who hit themselves in the side of the head.

The Big Scouser, however, had reminded the community that it was a bad idea to assume anything about anyone and that the guard should always be up. The experienced prison officers often said that the minute you become complacent was when 'something' happened.

# 10. NONCE

Fred, aged seventy, joined the magazine group and sat at the computer quietly writing poetry and short stories and making unconventional suggestions about articles.

'What about General James?' he said. 'I find that fascinating, don't you?'

General James was indeed fascinating, as a senior army medical officer who was found, on his death in 1865, to have been a woman named Miranda.

I directed the old man towards researching the history of Dartmoor, which he did with relish, ordering piles of books from the library, asking endless rather difficult questions about the various prisoners of war incarcerated over the years and voicing opinions about how badly they were treated.

He went red when I asked him what he was in for. Nothing had been right since his wife had died, he said. She had had a heart attack on the sofa. One minute she was there, the next she wasn't. He had been arrested for possessing indecent pictures of children.

There was awful sniggering in the classroom when somebody imitated the high pitched voice of Herbert in *Family Guy* – a joke which bypassed Fred, not only because he was deaf, but because the cultural reference was limited to the generation who had grown up watching Herbert 'the Pervert' attempt to seduce the young men of the Family Guy circle by luring them to his cellar with ice-lollies or drugging them with Tylenol PM.

Fred lived up to the Herbert joke by illustrating most of his articles, whatever they were about, with a picture of a semi-naked skinhead, and spent a long time on a review of the autobiography of the Olympic athlete Tom Daley, which contained several photographs of the young swimmer. Meanwhile the magazine group wondered why so many young men were seen going into Fred's cell; young men, in their opinion, who 'would have done anything for burn'.

Fred liked being in prison and he would be the first to admit it. Indeed, on the day of his departure, he had to be coaxed out of his cell.

'Leaving prison can be a very daunting challenge to some folk going out into the big wide word,' he wrote, as his release date loomed. 'This is especially true if you are in the older age group and are without family or friends outside. Even with good friends and a loyal family, there are still major issues that confront a man and cause fear and trepidation. The police and probation service are an active and vicious enemy to be confronted daily.'

For Fred the aged paedophile, vicious enemies lurked everywhere, although his fears seemed to diminish on his release, the details of which he sent to the magazine group in a letter describing the first week of his resettlement.

SUNDAY: Worried and fearful contemplating the future. How will I cope?

MONDAY: Said, Cheerio, and, Bye to folk. We wished each other well. Yesterday and today men came into the cell like vultures. Please may I have? I was pleased they felt free to ask. Always good to help someone else out. I was, and am, so grateful to the many folk who showed me such kindness and helpfulness during my imprisonment.

TUESDAY: The train was like a day trip. The past was like a dream. Enjoyed the journey.

WEDNESDAY: Had to report to probation. I was filled with fear and trepidation. Left home early on the first bus. Frightened of people. Had traditional English breakfast. Was disappointed with it, so accustomed to prison food. PROBATION! I am the first to criticise and complain but my probation officer is an excellent, helpful and considerate man. I consider myself well done by to be under his supervision.

THURSDAY: Quiet day. Walked up into town for shopping. No problems. What has amazed me is that nothing has come across as strange. Simply settled into daily routine. My one observation was the difficulty manouvering in crowds. A person is walking directly at you. How do you avoid a crash? My initial reaction is to stop and let them move around me. Got used to speed and distance. It's all coming together.

FRIDAY: Took public transport to next town. What amazed me was the vast amount of change. Shops closed, some new ones opened. People that you knew and used to work or interact with, now dead and gone. Found this day very nerve wracking. Felt very nervous and sensitive. Some old 'friends' no longer want to know me. Others take it in their stride.

SATURDAY: Finding life difficult to cope with. Only see the advantages of being inside. Visited my late wife's grave and cleaned the head stone. Later took an invalid neighbour out shopping. I became incredibly depressed at the end of this day but managed to comply with all aspects of my licence.

SUNDAY. Contemplating the visit tomorrow by police and probation at my home has filled with despair, despondency, depression and suicidal thoughts. I am like a zombie this evening. Unable to sleep and stressed out.

MONDAY: Day and visit went well. Both police and probation were helpful, considerate and supportive. An encouragement not to step out of line. Most of my fears, and yours, are nothing more than phantoms and shadows when we come to face them. Thanks and best wishes to all for the future.

Fred had been a lay preacher in the Baptist church. He was opinionated, infuriating, confused in his thinking, but rarely boring, and the insoluble contradictions of his personality were perhaps summed up by a member of his prayer group who, interviewed by a local newspaper, said on his arrest, 'I just don't understand why a person like that goes off the rails.'

The answer is that nobody really knows, including, more often than not, the happily married senior citizen who has been pronounced guilty as charged.

In 2013, when Jimmy Savile entered the canon of crime history as one of the UK's most prolific paedophiles, Operation Yewtree dragged its wide net along and caught various national treasures.

*Coronation Street* emptied as the male characters disappeared from the narrative with no explanation except for the vague allusion that they were 'in Germany'. It became evident that, while some cases were certainly down to the guilt of the accused, others were down to the insanity of the accuser. The scene was further discoloured by a murky socio-historical context, prosecutorial anomalies and the peculiarities that are incentivised by celebrity

Jeremy Wright MP, as Attorney General, boasted to the House of Commons that since the introduction of new guidelines in October 2013 the number of child abuse prosecutions had risen from 440 to 7,998 with a conviction rate of 76.2 per cent – 'The highest it has ever been.'

The dizzying number of successful prosecutions was doubtless aided by the fact that, as one lawyer observed in a letter to *Inside Time*, 'No evidence is required to convict on sexual offences,' because the Criminal Justice & Public Order Act 1994, the Sexual Offences Act 2003, and recent statutory amendments have combined to create a two-tier criminal justice system.

Where offences are theft, robbery and burglary the Prosecution is still obliged to prove 'beyond all reasonable doubt' that the defendant committed the offences. This still requires the corroboration of any verbal accusation, something tangible, to not only prove the offence but also to link the accused to the offence.

However, for sex offences, the Prosecution no longer has to prove 'beyond all reasonable doubt' that the offence occurred. The need for corroboration was removed by the Criminal Justice and Public Order Act 1994, Section 32 and 33.'

This, said the lawyer, 'Made false accusations not only possible but also more probable.'

The 'historical' sex offenders – men in their seventies and eighties –had lived normal educated middle-class white suburban lives – married, unmarried, employed, unemployed, retired, husbands, fathers, grandfathers.

They were usually teachers, often preachers. They were accused because their victims, having grown up, resented the reality of the damage done and sought accountability and/or compensation.

So the old men of the number proudly trumpeted by the Attorney General landed on a Prison Service ill-equipped to house them, let alone provide any kind of rehabilitative measure. They were placed in cells on the ground floor landings because so many were encumbered by debilitating conditions including, in more than one case, being blind. They ate their meals on trays laid on their beds as their ageing bodies struggled with most functions. They had to be looked after by a Buddy, another prisoner wearing a blue T-shirt. A volunteer in carpentry was deployed to build a ramp for the chapel.

It is easy to think of the paedophile as one simple stereotype – a dangerous delinquent who has no control over his compulsion to rape children and no regret when he has done so. The reality – in Dartmoor at least – was that sex offenders were a wide range of characters that had broken the law in a wide variety of ways and across a wide variety of age groups.

The 'nonce' could have cerebral palsy, dementia, a red woollen hat and roseacea. He could be the man making tiny teddy bears out of squished-up prison bread on B Wing. He could be the barman who swore he didn't know and the bloke who cried in the witness box. He was the rapist who could make you laugh out loud and the downloader who played the piano beautifully.

And he was Jeremy Forrest. The thirty-something teacher arrived famous, having received notoriety for 'abducting' one of his legally underage pupils and running away to France with her.

Hue, cry and arrest – Mr Forrest ended up on the wings with a five-and-a-half year sentence for child abduction. He was then the subject of a Channel 4 documentary entitled 'Sexting Teachers', which meant that he was the topic of gossip from the wings to staff rooms. 'Oi, mate, give us your autograph,' and so on.

The interesting thing about Jeremy Forrest was how uninteresting he was. A short thin man with jeans and glasses, his small features were on the cusp of pointed. In a place full of people who are often both nasty and gormless, he seemed to be neither, but what little charisma he had was entirely due to his notoriety; he played the guitar quite well, liked Nirvana. He was very ordinary, but a teenage girl had fallen in love with her teacher and the teacher had reciprocated. Plus he was in the middle of the socio-cultural whirlpool where Rolf Harris was guilty but serious questions were being asked about the legal age of consent.

Fame is not a friend to the prisoner. Jeremy Forrest was ghosted out of Dartmoor after a couple of months; he was said to be a troublemaker, sending in complaints and 'apps'. He didn't seem to be able to let go of his 'relationship' and fought for the right to remain in contact with his former lover. So out he went, in the van, through the fog, to HMP Channings Wood where, no doubt, he could swim largely in a small pond. He was released in 2015 to the predictable grainy long lens shots and newspaper adjectives about his gaunt appearance.

I wondered if he would publish a book to counter the book written (under a pseudonym) by his ex-girlfriend's mother and published by John Blake (the publishing company founded by an ex-Sun journalist). 'Davina Williams', though criticized for cashing in on her daughter's notorious 'abduction', nevertheless clearly laid out the two opposing schools of thought that tend to define the arguments around such cases. On the one hand the schoolgirl believes she is in love, that her 'affair' is cinematic in its romantic narrative, and that her Romeo is not a criminal but the man with whom she expects to spend the rest of her life, after walking up the aisle in a white meringue.

On the other hand the parents have been subjected to the anxiety of their child's illicit relations with a man who was supposed to occupy a trusted position and who, in the case of Jeremy Forrest, caused further misery by pleading Not Guilty and then failing to take the stand to explain himself. The police and Crown Prosecution Service are guided, of course, by the black and white of the law that states quite clearly what a fifteen-year-old should and should not be doing. Forrest, in the middle of this, certainly no hero, came across as a small man, confused, miserable, egocentric, and possibly encumbered by complex mental health issues that gave him an internal belief system at odds with the practical truths of real life.

The practical truths of real life also side-stepped Mr L, a minute individual on G Wing, who had denied his charge of indecent exposure on the grounds that his penis was so small he would have been ashamed to display it in case anyone laughed at him.

His case had been considerably enlivened by the arrival of a prostitute who told the court that Mr L had been a client of hers for twenty years and his append-age was of an average proportion.

Mr L was elderly and odd and obsessed with diggers. He hopped about on G Wing and played the drums in my music group for a bit. He told us that he was very good and had played in various famous '60s bands but, in fact, he had no sense of rhythm whatsoever. Literally none. It made the band furious and eventually I had to gently tell Mr L that other drummers 'wanted a go'.

Mr L seemed as harmless as the day is long, but he had offences dating back to 1977 and, in amongst the prostitutes and appendages, were the voices of those whose lives he had distorted. Mr L might seem harmless as an old man, but his past had been created when he was a young man.

A middle-aged mother told a local newspaper that the man had gone through life, 'Exposing himself, committing indecent acts, forcing children to commit indecency and using manipulation and, certainly in my case, violence, for his own sick self-gratification.

'He did not care about the destruction he has caused along the way. He has denied he has ever done wrong. He must have thought he was above the law or that no one would ever dare speak out. He was a very violent nasty person who committed some disgusting crimes against children.'

She said she was abused hundreds of times, then threatened and beaten to stop her speaking out.

'When you are constantly being told you are useless, ugly and worthless, you actually believe it to be the truth. From the age of fourteen to twenty I had cut myself on numerous occasions, half hoping to die. I had feelings of guilt and confusion. For years I would have flashbacks and nightmares but, slowly, time healed and I was as OK as I could be.'

Edward was in for downloading child porn. He was about thirty and had a history of violence. His eyes were small, green and cold and his angry thin lips pursed over a mouth overcrowded with small crouton teeth. He smelled dreadful. He sat in the corner of the classroom with a cover placed carefully over the computer that he had made his own. He said he didn't have much to do so I suggested he write an article about himself.

He described running away to King's Cross when he was fourteen and meeting a girl whose mother was a heroin addict. 'I wasn't sure what heroin was at that point, just that it was a drug.' They sold thrown away travel cards for money. 'We were making about £50 a night.' Then the girl bore a child by him and their daughter subsequently died of a brain tumour when she was eight. The girl married his cousin by whom she bore three more children. He went on to have two other children, a son and a daughter. There were also eleven dogs. This is England.

Things had started to go wrong when he was eight. 'I started hanging around with a lad called Tom and we would go to his uncle's flat. His uncle raped me.'

'After that things went bad for me. I got into trouble with the police for criminal damage, shoplifting and assault on a police officer, among other things. In 1995 I was accused of assault on a neighbour's daughter and as a result I was placed into care.'

At first I wondered if he was lying. Why? First of all because it is sensible to wonder this about any resident of HMP Dartmoor —many of them are liars and most of them want attention. But I was more confused by the tone of his life story. Violent incidents were told as black and white facts in a detached tone that had the effect of making them seem ordinary. No adjectives. No colour. No emotion.

'I walked out of the toilet her dad punched me in the face and dragged me into his bedroom before punching some more, he then spent the next two hours raping me.'

One of the other teachers sent up an alert. Worried emails circulated. There would be disclosure issues if the rapist had not been arrested. Could the writer handle writing his revelations?

I checked in.

'How are you coping with writing this story, in yourself I mean?'

'Oh,' he said in his matter of fact way. 'If it gets too much I take a break and play Solitaire.'

A few weeks later, on the wing, in one of the cluttered receptacles that constituted a temporary classroom, and alongside the objects of many other uses (cleaning equipment; discarded computer screen, unidentifiable plastic bits; exercise books) a tremor of emotion passed over his face as he pointed out that the day before had been the anniversary of his daughter's death.

It was difficult to see his face or connect with him because I was seated in a swivelling office chair which had broken and not only forced me to sit at some height above him but to concentrate on not falling off it.

He was on one of the low blue chairs. Would it come to me touching him? What happens if he breaks down?

He didn't break down; he was well protected by the cold armour of desensitisation – and there was no rational reason why he would show his vulnerability to me. After all, why should he?

'Do you have anyone here you can talk to?' I asked.

'Not really,' he shrugged. 'It helps speaking on the phone to my son.'

Edward left the prison and returned two years later. He had returned to his pattern of changing his name and he had breached his Sexual Offences Prevention Order by making friends with a teenage girl after beginning an affair with her mother.

The wheelchair-bound woman and her disabled 13-year-old daughter remained unaware of his past until his arrest. The mother later told a local newspaper that she had since been the target of abuse from vandals who scrawled 'kill paedo b****' on her front door.

Sentencing him to three more years in prison, the Recorder told him,

'Your behaviour is ingrained and you are a potential danger to children in society', adding: 'You wheedled your way into the life of the family who took you at face value, not knowing what sort of person you really are'.

Max looked angelic – and much younger than his twenty-four years. He arrived in the classroom, blond, educated. Small and rather beautiful, he looked as if he was about to be picked up by his parents from the quad at Marlborough College. He liked laughing and chatting and always had thoughtful contributions to make. He was in for assaulting an eleven year old.

He arrived in Dartmoor to find himself on the same wing as a man who had taught him at school; actually, to be more accurate, on the same landing, which in prison parlance makes a difference; the wing is your town – you don't know everyone on it; the landing is your street – you know most people on it, you're a neighbourhood, compelled to eat together, compelled to be locked down together if there is a staff shortage.

Asked what he would like to write about, Max revealed an interest in humanism about which he had read several books. He saw humanism as a stance that could be of interest to prisoners and wrote thus.

When people first come to prison it is usually a traumatic experience. Often a lot of people turn to religion as a means to help them cope. But a humanist would ask, 'Is this the rational path for people with troubles?

Humanism could help to give a perspective to a prisoner. It states that all are the same. Everybody is as capable of achievement and everybody is capable of making mistakes. Humanism can help create a better society. It encourages people to respect one another and themselves. Decisions are based around thought rather than faith, which would mean that some of the ideals that many people hold would be challenged, with the greater good in mind. It is an idea that helps you value other people and helps you to focus your own future and fulfil your own potential.

Humanists think for themselves rather than blindly accepting what they are told by figures of authority. This is because authority figures often have an agenda of their own, frequently the improvement of their own wealth or power. And even when this is not the case, authorities themselves can be uninformed or confused.

Arriving at prison, a sex offender is supposed to be availed of a 'sentence plan' which will include an assessment known as SARN (Structured Assessment of Risk and Need) which will allow him to transfer to a 'treatment-centred ethos.' The treatment-centred ethos is a specialised prison, such as HMP Wayland, where there is clinical provision such as an SOTP (Sex Offenders' Treatment Programme).

The SOTP was introduced in 1991 and has various guises but it is basically a course that includes both cognitive behaviour therapy and exercises in 'victim empathy'. The underlying point is to enable the offender to take responsibility for his crime and make the behavioural changes necessary to persuade the parole board that he is no longer a risk to the public.

Sometimes the paedophile will agree to take prescribed drugs, or pharmacotherapy, as is known in the language of the 'biological psychiatrist'. In HMP Whatton, a prison in Nottingham, measures have included SSRIs and anti-androgens. The SSRI (Fluoxetine and so on) is believed to interact with testosterone in the regulation of sexual behaviour. The anti-androgen is seen to moderate sex drive.

The development, delivery and evaluation of sex offender programmes tend to fall in the domain of those who work in the fields of forensic psychology and criminology. Hampered by limited access to prisoners, or prisons, the findings of researchers are condemned to remain obscure. Where a report does appear it is rendered in the language of the peer review, where a 'grievance-motivated sexual murderer' has become a 'catathymic gynocide' and 'recovery' can be an 'emergent paradigm'.

Academics and physicians write reports and make proposals but neither the under-resourced prison or the sex offender or his victims or the yous and mes who foot the bill benefit from suggestions made by researchers, reformers or politicians because their proposals are so often only ideas. Ideas have a mercurial relationship with operational reality. They can land like a bee on the wrong flower and cause no consequence largely because prison budgets decrease and, even if they didn't, nobody is going to prioritise the rehabilitation of (or anything else for) paedophiles.

Useful information is slow to filter down to the frontline where practical help is desperately needed, so sex offenders do not see the light of day. They are cast into darkness and, as a consequence, most of them, aged and Caucasian, are left to die, slowly and expensively.

Serves them right, says the mob. But not enough is known about this haggard tribe. They are dismissed. The last lepers, untouched even by the political rectitude of the right-on brigade, which means that they (and more importantly their criminal sexuality) remain hidden from the laboratory light that is shed on the other mysteries of mental health and human behaviour.

Dartmoor, despite housing hundreds of sex offenders, did not provide a Sex Offender Treatment Programme and there was an eighteen-month waiting list to obtain a position on one in other prisons. So even the paedophiles who were appalled by their compulsions and desperate for help were unlikely to get it.

Prisoners could sometimes access an A–Z 'short motivational programme' that aimed to give offenders the opportunity to think about their lives. This was based on something called the 'Good Lives Model' and was seen to be 'a mechanism within which positive behaviours can be encouraged.' It was also designed to engage the so-called Refusers and Deniers.

Refusers are those who have admitted to the crime for which they have been incarcerated, but are refusing to participate in behaviour modification programmes targeted at sex offenders. This might be because they don't want to address the issue through fear of bringing unwelcome emotions to the surface.

Deniers are those who claim they are innocent in spite of their charges and, therefore, do not see that the programmes bear any relevance to them. For a Denier, participation in a sex offending programme might harm their appeals, as it would make them appear guilty of a crime they are claiming they did not commit.

Deniers are Mr T, who says he is not guilty but he has already served four years which, he points out, has cost the taxpayer £45,000 times four. This high estimate reflected Mr T's innumerable health conditions and the expenses incurred as he was taxied to and from Derriford Hospital. He was, 'Quite happy in the warm with three meals a day'. Nevertheless he continued to appeal in the legal (and no other) sense of the word.

'Who's going to refund me for the loss of me house?' he asked me. 'David Cameron and all that lot? He always passes the buck to the Democrat or whatever 'e is.'

We, as civilian staff, underwent 'grooming' and 'corruption' training to alert us to the manipulative ways of the sex offender and how to be on our guard against them —even instructors who had been in the prison for years said that relationships with prisoners were a 'minefield'. Particularly in this isolated part of Devon, where everyone knew each other and you could easily be in the pub and be asked by a prisoner's relation how so and so was doing.

Our instructor, an approachable prison governor, opened the session by admitting his own failings, thus reminding us that to be humane was to be human, but to be humane was to be fallible and fallibility in a secure setting was to attract unseen and unpredictable consequences. What, he asked, did we think were the main reasons for corruption? Mobile telephones? Drugs? Money? No. Love.

Love! This could mean people having sex in the stationery cupboard, but it could also mean the kind-hearted prison officer who was sacked because, on posting a birthday card for a prisoner, it ended up at the home of the young daughter that same prisoner had raped.

It's a sick picture, but it is not rendered in black and white, it has many colours and they make a landscape that confuses even the most seasoned professionals. This was highlighted on the day that the Prison Service banned page 49 of *Inside Time*.

*Inside Time*, a charity funded newspaper written for prisoners, is widely circulated and widely read by some 100,000 people in the prison system. It is, to Democracy's credit, usually left alone and, over the years, has become a platform for prisoners to complain about their depressing and nonsensical narrative, a place for penal reformers to vent and for solicitors to advertise. However, on this occasion, the April edition of the newspaper had been printed and prison governors were asked to remove some pages because they contained 'inappropriate' images.

Those of *Inside Time* who had allowed the pictures to be a part of the 'Book Highlight' pages were mystified by the constraint. Those who read *Inside Time* were, of course, extremely interested in what had been displayed on the missing page 49.

The answer was a story about a book entitled, *Tippi: My book of Africa* whose, "magical images chronicle the life of Tippi Degre who was brought up with wild animals..." The photographs showed, "the young girl making friends with an elephant who she calls her brother and a leopard, her best friend."

This was judged to be material that could stimulate sinister arousal, so page 49, meerkats and semi-naked child, bows and arrows and Namibian bushmen, were all ripped out, leaving *Inside Time* editors mystified and prisoners sending in disgruntled letters to the Number One Governor.

## 11. THE LITTLE FELLA

The individual who appeared in Plymouth Crown Court six months after his victim bled out on the prison's kitchen floor did not look like a killer. Tall and grim maybe, but depressing rather than frightening. Known on the wings as 'Scouser Bill' his head had been shaved to make a greyish pink dome. His eyes were hidden behind a pair of oval-rimmed glasses in which there were tinted purple lenses, so his expression was hidden. His eyes in the old black and white photograph of his face produced by Google Images were those of dark anger and serious threat; in his past he had looked dangerous. Now, at the age of fifty, he looked like literally anyone.

Expressionless, he sat behind glass, thin lips stuck together in an immobile hyphen, he lurked, like so many long-term prisoners, passive behind the defence barrier he had built for himself and which had served to help protect him against the danger he had faced over the years he had served in prison for bludgeoning his girlfriend to death in 1996.

The murder of Kathy Sharples, in a bathroom in a flat in Newquay, was the subject of some legal discussion amongst the ten lawyers gathered to perform the prosecution and the defence. At the age of thirty-six and addicted to heroin Tolcher had murdered Kathy then stolen her jewellery and gone to the post office to cash her benefit cheque.

Tolcher was claiming that he was innocent of this first murder. His defence strategy, according to his lawyer, was that he would attempt to persuade the court that, as he was innocent of this killing, so too he was innocent of the current one. Somebody else had done them in both cases, and in both cases he had been framed by the real perpetrator. In the case of the murder of 'Cuzzy' in Dartmoor, he had been framed by a nameless assassin who had intimidated eye-witnesses to cover up for him. The prisoners who were to be called to testify about what they had seen were liars.

It seemed to be an optimistic gamble, but Scouser Bill was adamant in his Not Guilty plea, with the consequence that twenty people had been employed to process his defence in a court case that went on for four days and was of little interest to anyone apart from myself, one journalist from the local *Plymouth Herald*, and Alexander Cusworth's mother, Ann Edgeller, who sat in the public gallery with tears running down her face.

Here was one murder committed by a violent man on another violent man, both warehoused out of sight and out of mind. It was not nearly exciting enough to warrant a position in national news – the death of a homeless and chaotic junkie living off the state was of little consequence in the reality of many vaster tragedies.

As the crime reporter from the *Plymouth Herald* said outside on the steps, 'No one cares about this one because it was in a prison.'

But I had spent three years in the warehouse with men like Alex Cusworth. They were real to me. I had not known him personally, partly because he could not read or write, and was therefore unlikely to graduate towards writing for pleasure. But I had known many like him because his case history resonated with the universal facts of so many prisoners' existences. Abuse. Anger. Drugs. Violence.

Fury lurked on all the wings ready to erupt at any time. It was part of the everyday reality of this working environment where staff briefings detailed the lives of endless forgotten and dehumanised people, many of whom said, again and again, that they had nothing to live for; many of whom were cutting themselves, killing themselves and screaming for help in a place where there were no ears because there were no staff because there was no money.

Any week in any prison could produce a Mr A who informed night patrol that he had swallowed razor blades and there was blood in his urine; a Mr G who had smeared blood over his wall, face and arms and then handed the razor to the night duty officer; a Mr H, who, having returned from an AA meeting, took 170 Paracetamol tablets; a Mr S who cut his left arm and stated he was 'bored'. When I first arrived a Mr M cut his own toe off. We were told it could be found in the fridge in the Mandatory Drug Testing Unit. If anyone happened to be looking for it.

Assaults tended to be prisoner on prisoner or prisoner on prison officer, rather than on the women who tended to be the teachers, drug workers and counsellors. But you never knew because, as the Big Scouser had proved on that afternoon, fatal acts are completely unpredictable; any one of 1,000 people could have been killed on that day, and every one of those 1,000 people knew it. The sensible did not dwell on it; they could not if they were to continue delivering the service they had chosen to provide, but there it was. A big knife and an erratic killer.

'Alex,' said Simon Laws, who was prosecuting, 'had no chance.'

Dartmoor was not alone in its grim circumstance, but part of a greater picture where statistics were sounding alarm amongst those who are paid with public money to take responsibility for the welfare of the prison state. The same week that Tolcher took the stand in Plymouth Crown Court the Queen took her place in Parliament and gave a speech where her Government promised that prison reform would be the centrepiece of their agenda.

The Ministry of Justice had published a report that had stimulated what appeared to be genuine concern amongst those running the country. Michael Gove, then Minister of Justice, was being quoted in the newspapers about his commitment to reform following the publication of a bulletin that stated that suicides in prison were up from seventy-nine deaths a year to a hundred. There had been 32,313 incidents of self-harm (up by twenty-five per cent from the previous year). Assaults numbered 20,518, with escalations in attacks on prisoners (up twenty-four per cent) and on staff (up thirty-six per cent).

Here, then, was the actual statistic. One murder, reflecting the myriad aspects of ordinary criminality portrayed in all its mundane reality – unromantic, unglamorous, banal, expensive. Just an ugly incident that was outlined in minute detail over the next four days in Room 3, a functional space in a modern crown court building in the middle of Plymouth.

William Tolcher had served time in prisons all over the United Kingdom, with a spell at the high security Whitemoor amongst others. He had been assaulted more than once by other prisoners over the years and had fought back, in one case throwing boiling water over another prisoner and stabbing him in the hand with a pen.

He ended up on D Wing at Dartmoor, a prison that was familiar to him because he had been there in the 1980s and '90s. He was given a job in the kitchen and access to a twenty-three-inch knife for chopping vegetables.

The jury was availed of a colour dossier full of evidence which included a computer generated 3D colour illustration of the trajectory of the knife pushed into Alex Cusworth's body and the injuries sustained by his internal organs.

The making of tea was explained as a process that employed twenty-seven men in a busy industrial kitchen where jobs were coveted, not only because it allowed the indiscriminate gobbling of stolen food, but because there was the possibility of gaining an NVQ qualification in, for instance, food handling.

Alexander Cusworth was pleased that he got this job and had rung his mum to tell her the good news. The small wage (around £10 a week) would pay for extras. He might get an NVQ. Things might get better. His mother had felt quite hopeful after the phone call, and hope had become something of a luxury in the life of her adopted son.

As the prisoners in the kitchen prepared curried eggs for tea, three members of the prison staff were holding a meeting in a side room, which did not provide them with a view to the proceedings. Tolcher had been in Dartmoor for only a matter of months, but had worked in the kitchens there and at other prisons before. Three knives had been signed out to him so that the food preparation team could chop vegetables.

The hour, 3 p.m., would be familiar to anyone with prison experience as a natural break in the middle of the afternoon: teachers would escape to the staff room to have a cup of tea; prisoners would walk around the yard with their shirts off if they could get away with it; others would smoke an illegal cigarette in the loo.

I had always honoured this break as important, at the very least, to my own sanity. I supplied biscuits to the learners who came to Creative Writing and Magazine Production. Biscuits (as food) were on the Prohibited List, a Class C item along with tobacco, money, clothing, drink, letters, paper, books, tools, and information technology equipment. You were not allowed to bring them in. They weren't as bad as Class A, guns and drugs, but I was told that people had been fired for bringing in biscuits. I didn't care, they could 'walk me out' of the prison for bringing in chocolate digestives if they wanted. It was a risk I was willing to take. If nothing else, it would bring to light one of the many nonsensical and grotesquely reductive anomalies of prison life.

I had noticed that the younger guys became more agitated when their blood sugar fell and I saw supermarket custard creams as a simple way to address the possibility that they could become unnecessarily volatile. Furthermore it was during the tea break, an informal respite, when people tended to relax and speak the truth about their lives and the lives of others and the members of the group got to know each other.

It was a time for 'sharing,' a moment when it was most likely that information about the real issues would be aired – sometimes as gossip, sometimes as real anxiety. It was when S showed me the marks on his wrists after his girlfriend dumped him and when A told me how he had been recalled to prison after smoking a legal high, when P described how he had been attacked in his cell when three people jumped him, and D described a similar assault, for no other reason than because he was gay. B had been threatened with death, when (in a polite middle-class accent) he asked a thief to return the tin of tuna he knew he had stolen from his cell. They talked about their children, their lawyers, and their lives on the wings – when so and so had found a shit on the stairs, when L had been sent back to G Wing after dropping a piece of bacon on a sex offender's head and then all the televisions had gone down and there had nearly been a riot.

The tea break was important, but it was also the moment when the eye could be taken off the ball. In my case, my learners would wander off into other classrooms and annoy both the teachers and their learners with pointless provocation or there would be climbing over partitions to retrieve paper aeroplanes and doctoring puzzles with hidden rude words, but it was all secondary modern rather than sinister sociopathy, smoking cigs and idiotic banter rather than assault and battery.

3 p.m. was the moment William Tolcher walked around to Alex Cusworth's workstation and pushed a blade deep into his side for reasons that, despite the four days in court, and several witness statements, remained unknown.

Why wasn't there CCTV in the kitchen? the jury wondered. 'Money' was the Catering Manager's answer on the second day.

The jury was told there had been no conversation between Tolcher and Cusworth immediately before the attack, so it was assumed the victim had said something earlier that Tolcher had taken offence to.

Tolcher could not reveal anything because he was pleading innocence. The prisoners who came to testify had only seen glimpses of the drama; one had seen the big Scouser pull the knife out of Alex; another had heard him say, 'You won't fucking talk to me like that,' while a third told the police that Tolcher had said to him, 'I have just fucked up, I have fucked up big. I have stuck a ten-inch blade into Alex.'

William Tolcher took the stand on the third day. He said he had not murdered Alex, he did not know who had, and he could not understand why the witnesses were lying about what they had seen. Furthermore he had not murdered Kathy Sharples; he had loved her.

Tolcher's internal processes remained unfathomable. Having denied the murder of his girlfriend for several years, he had then confessed to it to a psychiatrist in prison. Why? Because, he told the court, he wanted parole, he wanted to see his children, and admission to the offence was the only way to get it.

The afternoon that Alex Cusworth had died was like any other, he told the jury in his flat Liverpudlian accent. He was chopping onions with another prisoner then he had put his knife down on the table and gone to the locker room for a cigarette. The inference was that the other prisoner had taken the knife, committed the crime, and returned the knife. The next thing Tolcher knew was that they were all being told to move to the back of the room because somebody had been stabbed.

It was at this point, at round 12 noon, that I thought Tolcher had provided reasonable doubt. The twenty or so kitchen workers had spent five hours together, corralled in the locker room, talking about the incident. There was certainly time to form a story that would send Tolcher down and protect the real killer depending on the power and intelligence of the real killer. The staff had not seen anything, and certainly had not seen what had happened with the knife. Tolcher was a self-confessed loner with no friends but very little was known about the other characters who were in the kitchen at the same time as him; prison has its own reality and I wondered if he had been set up by a cabal about whom we knew nothing.

The prisoners who gave evidence had records in the public domain as liars, but they had not been offered any 'inducements' (such as early release, or privileges) to cooperate with the investigation. Their evidence was realistically unclear, as evidence would be in describing five seconds that, as one of them said, had seemed like a lifetime. But, they said, they wanted to do the right thing by Alex. No one deserved that. 'Whatever happens I can't justify how a guy died that day. All I can do is help with what I've seen.'

I was alone in my moment of reasonable doubt. The jury went out for two hours and returned with a guilty verdict.

The judge, Mr Justice Dingemans, imposed another life sentence and told Tolcher he would serve at least thirty-three years before he could apply for parole. 'You are an extremely dangerous man,' he said. 'And a complete stranger to the truth.'

Ann Edgeller read out an impact statement to the jury, 'My son,' she said, 'was a very vulnerable young man with mental health issues who never got the help that he deserved.'

## 12. THE ROCKY ROAD TO REDEMPTION

The Creative Writing sessions, like the Art sessions, allowed prisoners to embark on the personal processes that are required if a person is to change, and change was, after all, the goal. The Number One governor certainly thought so. During a visit to the magazine group a prisoner asked her what qualities she thought were required to make a good governor. She answered that she thought humility was important ('No-one gets everything right all of the time') and a belief in redemption ('Everyone can change should they choose to do so.')

Humility and redemption are the words of religions rather than Civil Service instruction, but they are resonant nonetheless, loaded with echoes of prisons past and present, where miscreants have to acknowledge their defects and redeem themselves, both to themselves and to the society that has judged them.

B thought about this a lot. He knew he had to because he had damn nearly destroyed the family (a wife and two young children) that he adored. He knew he had caused chaos and confusion, that his children were too young to understand, and that it was important for him to become the parent they deserved if he was to earn his second chance.

'Prison gives us time to think,' he wrote. 'How did we get here? And what can we do to make sure we never come back? Things have to change. You have to change and be seen to change.'

Very clever, middle-class, and in for fraud, he had been a professional and successful screenwriter before landing on F Wing where, because he was a writer, his imagination and detachment allowed him to take pleasure in his own observations, in the absurd oscillations of prison life and in the unbelievable characters that roamed the wings. He believed that the study of these characters could lead to some useful answers about what it was that separated the recidivist from the person who achieved the successful atonement required of a new start.

'We can leave prison unreconstructed,' he wrote, 'but it's not good for the soul or the best use of the one thing we've all got plenty of: time. Every one of us deserves the opportunity of redemption in life for the things that we've done that weren't great. But what is redemption? I'm not talking about 'Him' upstairs, St Peter and the pearly gates. I'm talking about what we can do to make things right in this life, not in the next.

'For me this was pleading guilty at the earliest opportunity. I took the view that when you're nicked, you're nicked. I knew what I had done wrong. And while I disagreed with why the police thought I did it, pleading guilty allowed me to take ownership of what I had done wrong and to begin to forgive myself.

'It would be a criminal waste of a human life to be judged only for the worst thing we've ever done. But if we don't achieve some kind of redemption inside, how will society accept that we have paid their price in full and let us get on with the rest of our lives?'

Richard, in for violence, out in three years time, had an epiphany. He felt as if he had been personally touched by the love of the Lord, or something, and it changed his life. Calm, spiritually awakened, if you will, he felt blessed.

Richard was the chapel orderly, a coveted job and one that was given out carefully as it required maturity, commitment and enough physical strength to move the altar out of the way when senior management come in to announce their various intentions and attempt to operate their Power Point presentations.

He spent his days sitting at a little desk in the chapel vestry reading books about Christianity and writing notes on lined paper in Biro. His path of investigation included the *Book of Jeremiah*, and *Becoming Free Through Meditation and Yoga*. And he was very keen on Paul Coelho, enjoying *The Valkyries* as an inspirational message about forgiving the past and believing in the future.

Around him, in his monkish enclave, were the signs of the work of the chaplaincy – a filing system for Sikhs, a window sill full of Virgins and a cross or two, pictures of Jesus sermonising, as well as an iron, a Hoover, a CD player, several electric guitars, and newspapers such as *The War Cry*, for the Salvation Army, and *Muslim News* with the headline, '570 Children Killed in Israel's Indiscriminate Bombing of Gaza'.

Practical commitment superseded any semblance of unctuous religiosity. He had to sweep up rats' droppings, clean the loo where smokers puffed out of the extractor fan, count the sugar sachets, as everybody always thought the chapel wouldn't miss a few, count the ceramic mugs because prisoners hated the blue plastic ones and only Enhanced were allowed china.

He worked from 8.30 a.m. – 4.00 p.m. and enjoyed the company, as everyone visited the chapel at one time or another. Governors came to give out certificates for education, prisoners sat quietly with a candle, the Independent Monitoring Board talked about Seg, Buddhists discussed their moments, the Sunday choir sang hymns.

He had come to believe that the soul is eternal and affected by deeds past and present. The soul, he thought, was moulded by a person's behaviour because it was subject to spiritual laws that were as precise as the laws of science. Thus he was learning how to find meaning in everyday reality, interest in invisibility, and company in those who have asked the big questions so many times.

Richard was convinced about his findings, convinced about the loving power of a greater being, and he wished that everyone could feel the same as he did. They didn't, of course and, though it was difficult for Richard not to evangelise about his true path, he remained aware that there were many true paths, despite his conviction that his was the right one.

Another prisoner, Mick, in with a short sentence, was an atheist but, as he pointed out, this did not mean that he was either opposed to organised religions or that he believed in nothing at all. In fact he believed that all problems could be overcome with 'compassion and understanding'. He just didn't go for the 'power of prayer' when he was at his lowest ebb, and wondered why this method was only offered when you were at your most vulnerable.

'Not subscribing to a religion does not take away my inherent belief in humanity and love. Not believing in an interpretation of a god makes it impossible for me to argue with a different interpretation, let alone hate or even kill those who disagree with me.'

Education offered functional skills where you could learn to add up; the library offered a book group where you could read *Kes*; the wings offered opinions about television and football, but the chapel was a place where philosophical ideas could be discussed with other people interested in the matters of the soul and mind. And, open to all, it was free of doctrine or dogma and allowed prisoners to pick and choose their own paths on the rocky road to redemption.

Colin thought of the prison chapel with affection, and wrote about his experiences as a young offender.

'I went to the chapel quite a few times not to go to services but to chill and see the chaplains. They done groups on evening association so I'd go up there with a few others. It was good because outside people would come in from some service provider and come and talk to us and ask us how we are and what it's like in prison for us.

The chapel done Bible studies, nothing too heavy, but rosary beads were massive in YOs and in order to get the different colours you had to do the studies. It was really good – it was a way of making Christianity attractive to young people and commit people to doing some study, as a way of at least introducing religion to them, sometimes for the first time ever.

I got all the colours white, black, baby blue, navy blue, brown, pink, yellow, orange, red, purple, green and glow in the dark. I'm pretty sure that was all of them. In some cases

I managed to get more than one colour so I used to sell them for burn or give them to friends when I was out.

Girls in rosaries are fit especially with a Croydon facelift which was a common way for girls to have their hair back then. I wouldn't know if this is still the case though, obviously, being as I can't see through walls.

I loved it, going to the chapel, and I firmly believe that to attract new people to Christianity (and religions in general) more needs to be done to spice it up and to show people the relevance that religion has in their every day, ungodly, materialised lives – show people the significance and relevance no matter how small it is.

I think they need to glamorise religion to a certain extent like a shiny pair of rosaries then people are gonna be like what's this all about? That would look wicked on me! What free! I'm getting involved! They should promote it get one at every service like over Christmas or hand them out at midnight mass and little statues and that but I don't know. I do believe more can be done though.'

Deities of various types have long been welcome in the prison system. One of the first Lords, He of Christianity, appeared at the gates of historical prisons in the form of the parish priest, who evolved into the probation officer. The priest met the errant member of the local flock and returned him to his parish where, with food, prayer and forgiveness, he was guided towards the 'correct' path.

The Quaker Lord, meanwhile, can be thanked for moving prison reform forward in the form of Elizabeth Fry, while Arthur Koestler's humanist approach, though eschewing any Lords, is still alive in the consequential arts awards that he founded and which still display the talents of the men inside many years after the philosopher's suicide.

Prison Service Instruction 51/2011 informed governors that twenty denominations have been passed for practice in prison. These are: Baha'i, Buddhism, Christianity, Christian Science, the Church of Jesus Christ of Latter Day Saints (Mormons), Hinduism, Humanism, Islam, Jainism, Jehovah's Witnesses, Judaism, Paganism, Quakerism, Rastafari, Seventh Day Adventist Church, Sikhism, Spiritualism, and Zoroastrianism.

This is a spectacular pantheon. A veritable catwalk of entities can trip the light fantastic of a prisoner's inner life and with them comes the cabinet of curiosities that are the regalia of ritual and worship that are allowed to be kept by prisoners as part of their 'prop' (property) and are not confiscated should their cells be 'spun'.

Buddhists can have a Buddha; Christians can have a Bible; Hindus have their Mala (prayer beads), Gita (holy book), and Murti (statue); Muslims have prayer mats and miswak sticks; Pagans are allowed wands and Rastafarians can hang the Lion of Judah flag but are (unsurprisingly) forbidden from the smoking of 'sacramental' cannabis.

The chaplaincy diary, printed once a month, also reflected a multidisciplinary approach which included the delegation of Holy Days to Dhamma, the commemoration of various imams, the Earth Birthday of His Majesty Haile Selassie, and Eid, amongst many others.

Everyone takes the Mick, of course. The papers had a field day when they found out about the Pagans' wands and pentacles. Meanwhile the prisoners converted to Mormonism in order to get free hot chocolate and went to Sunday services to get off the wings and enjoy the music.

Colin converted to Islam, briefly, and was watched by 'security' as he carried his new prayer mat around the prison and ostentatiously studied the Koran. He insisted he wasn't being radicalised by his new best friend, a Muslim who was in prison for rape.

I knew he was vulnerable, being clever, auto-didactic, sensitive, disenfranchised, very alone and very bored. I had understood the significant depths of Colin's boredom the day that he told me that he considered going to hospital to be a good day out.

'I've been to hospital on numerous occasions and I love it every time,' he insisted. 'I used to fake overdoses to get days out at hospital. I'd take ten paracetamol, show them evidence that I took forty then go to hospital. I take some because if you're found to be lying and have nothing in your system staff nick you for obstruction, but if there's some, say, ten, not enough to OD but enough to show up, then you won't get nicked.'

Although usually self-aware and articulate, he didn't have any very good reason for reading the Koran beyond it was something to do and he had done everything else and the food was good at Ramadan.

'That's all fine, Colin,' I said. 'But be very, very careful.'

Sometimes I wondered if Colin's maverick decisions were to do with a subconscious fear of getting out of prison and, occasionally, I told him I thought this. He looked as if he had heard but you never knew. He always took the most provocative path he could, and the provocative path did not lead either to healthier risk assessments or to resettlement in society. He was institutionalised, home was prison; there was no life outside, the friends long gone, the mother ill, the sister in touch but a stranger.

I saw his interest in Allah as both a genuine desire to find a meaningful structure to his inner life, which was full and colourful, and to take a legitimised rebel stance.

Islam was a good way to stick two fingers up at authority, made more gratifying by the fact that the authority had to allow it to happen because it was Religion and subject to all the coda of human rights laws.

If he had been converting to Buddhism all would have been well, and he could have converted to Buddhism as it was, as he would have put it, 'on offer'. Everyone liked Buddhism, it was a popular religion, the meditation was soothing with the incense and biscuits, and the discussion groups gave meaning to mindfulness. But Colin chose Allah, and enjoyed his regular arguments with the imam about the various points of doctrine, reporting on their details with interest and enthusiasm, which meant, at least, that nothing was covert. Everybody talked about it with him, particularly after he knelt down and faced Mecca in the tea-room.

'What the fuck's he doing?'

'It's Muslim innit.'

The chapel and the space that it created was the heart of the prison. It was where humans and humanity were allowed and encouraged, where prisoners cried when they lost their mums and where they went when they had self-harmed and everyone was laughing at the bandages in the gym. And it was where the mums rang when they were terrified for the safety of their sons, which was often.

It was good for books and quiet sessions with sympathetic people who did not judge you because you groped your niece in 1982. The Anglican Chaplain was young, attractive and smiley and she cared. Caring is a precious commodity in this bleak domain of toothless neediness and illegal desires. Caring needs to be cultivated. Caring and thinking can grow in the silence that graces the space of the chapel, except on music group nights when the feedback was quite loud and various murderers were murdering *House of the Rising Sun*.

Everyone needs to be quiet occasionally, to chill. Sometimes it was simply the noise of the wings that made men feel mad, sometimes it was missing the kids. The chapel allowed the time to think. Work things out. Grieve. Breathe.

I have no specific Lord myself but, like most civilians staggering about in this terrain, I have been burdened by a social conscience, or vocation; a deep need to divert the attention from myself to others in the knowledge that dwelling on the self is the unrighteous road to despair.

The civilian who has decided (by mistake) to be of service to others must leave self-interest at the door of the prison. Self-interest but not ambition – ambition to collect better resources, to raise funds to provide a wider range of sensibly targeted activities – ambition to address the depressing demands of bureaucracy and security and ambition to help prisoners achieve goals and develop their potential. All of which is very difficult, the day-to-day reality being so grim. The rank stench of total pointlessness often seeped into my nostrils and remained there long after the last key had been handed over and the car was racing home across the misty moor.

The challenging days were not usually caused by the prisoners, but by my own moods. Introspective and introvert, I had to consciously practise putting my own inner reality aside in order to be a professional in a place where the way one behaved was of inestimable importance. Many prisoners had no experience of either mature or professional behaviours so I did my best to be sensible, generous, tolerant, patient and boundaried. Furthermore it was really important to both show respect and gain it, because gaining it meant that I could put the potential for danger to one side and work with larger groups that would occasionally listen to me, even if I did sometimes have to stand on a table and shout.

I never looked for thanks or gratitude, firmly believing it a mistake to do so; the job was not anyone's choice but my own. I was not there to be thanked. I had chosen to be paid to deliver a service in the hope that service would have a positive effect. Occasionally, however, a prisoner would write a piece that reflected on my contribution to their personal world. AB was one. A substance misuser with no control over his habit, he managed to articulate the effect that creative writing had had on him, and I was grateful he had done so because it allowed me to acknowledge there was a small point to what I was doing.

'I started writing about 2 to 3 years ago at HMP Dartmoor. Maybe it was because I came to prison, again, a feeling sorry for myself kind of attitude, can my life get any more repetitive? No matter what choices I make I always end up making the extreme ones, the sometimes life changing ones, or was it because I see so many bullshitters and fake people and now I'm being forced to act like I'm someone I'm not. I felt that I was trapped in someone else's world, unable to be heard by the real world, isolated, alone and despairing.

And so I found the written word. Its therapeutic qualities, soothed my mind, releasing the pressure from the cooker of things that should have been said, and would have been said, if only I had more courage to be real to myself and stayed focused.

Writing has freed me from my mind now, I can actually express myself much better maybe that's because I can slow down and find that focus, so I'm not as frustrated as I once was. I have life experience on my side now to help me in making better decisions. From now I am going to try at least to practice what I preach.

I have found as I have gone past the frustrating writer's blocks or countless screwed up bits of paper, I have got much better at writing. I have crafted what I would like to think of as my style of expression.

I look forward to the creative writing sessions. They helped to keep me sane in an insane environment, to put the mighty pen to paper and come out of it smarter, faster and with a whole load more self belief.'

Prison is a complicated place. Complicated for reasons I could not foresee when I arrived in 2012 and which only came to light as a direct result of my experience in it.

After three years I knew some of the prisoners very well and I was genuinely fond of them, but affection has no place in this domain, and love has to adapt to a set of unclear socio-dynamics whose vagaries are invisible and unpredictable.

How does a woman love a man in prison without disrupting the status quo? How to love the sex offender from behind sky-high boundary walls? Why love the sex offender? And by love I do not mean having sex with them. I mean considering their needs, hoping to provide a service that will help them go forward in a positive way, without judging them, or being revolted, or any of the other responses that characterises the majority of their social interactions.

As the Number One Governor so clearly put it, everyone can change should they choose to do so. You don't go to work in a prison in a civilian or vocational capacity without having some faith in the truth of this premise.

Sex and love, love and sex, move around as invisible energies amongst unloved and untouched men. The prisoner is not your friend, this message comes over loud and clear and quickly, both in training and with common sense and in the way that the majority of them treat you. Everyone is after something because most of them have nothing and all are living in an impoverished institution that reinforces the idea that they deserve nothing.

At the most simple I was a teacher and/or an employer, so I was bound by the invisible coda of these identities. I had provided a magazine for them to learn how to publish. I had found resources to publish a book of their stories. I had provided sessions that were conducive to creative thought, and I had provided some respite from the dull, dehumanising rigmarole.

I had had some teacher training, but teacher training is designed for those who will teach adult learners of the civilian population, not adult learners who have been on heroin for five years, have been raped by the teacher of their youth, who left school at thirteen, whose inner life may feel uncontrollable and demonic, who may have withdrawal symptoms, psychotic episodes, fear, shakes, sweats, or may be simply subsumed by a deep misery they cannot articulate.

'They've told me I got a multiple personality disorder,' said one talented member of the magazine group.

'I'm ADHD, I can't do the washing up,' was another announcement, whilst one prisoner proudly said to me,

'I think I might be a psychopath.' To which my response was, 'Don't be silly, you're not a psychopath.' To which his answer was, 'Well, if I was a psychopath, you wouldn't know, would you?'

It was difficult to know how to be close and helpful rather than close and triggering aspects of a personality about which one knew nothing but were rooted in the experiences of the man rather than the actuality of his relationship with the member of staff.

Staff themselves, in particular, young female prison officers, were often caught up in the complexities of chronic loneliness; they saw the man and not the crime and sometimes they fell in love with him, or had sex with him, or both. Not in Dartmoor particularly, but in other prisons. And they were immediately fired for it, rather than supported with advice as to how to manage the unruly semi-feral mob that stared open-eyed and silently at their tits.

One teacher reported a prisoner for hugging her – he had meant it as a spontaneous act of affection, but she didn't know that he was in for dealing drugs. He could have been a rapist. I managed to avoid hugging, though it was not always easy. I tended to shake

prisoners' hands when they wanted to express gratitude or when they were leaving, which was the most
overtly emotional moment you had with them.

'I hope I never see you again,' was my stock response
to a prisoner on his departure. Although I did see them
again quite often because they came back. They were
always coming back.

Towards the end of my residency, and after the
murder of Alex Cusworth, I began to feel not unsafe,
exactly, but more unsure of myself, and if there is one
thing you need in your arsenal on this battlefield it is
self-confidence.

I didn't want working relationships that were
moulded by neediness or missing mum or missing any
woman, or hating them for that matter. I wanted to
produce published work written by men who understood the privilege of having the space and time to
produce that work. But the challenges presented by the
prisoners' personalities started to become the lesson,
and it was not one for which I was prepared with
information. I did not want to fuck with anyone's
head, though, because I knew them, I so often had very
strong opinions about their truths – when they were
being dishonest, when they were being selfish, when
they were being facile, when they were being rude,
when they were being attention-seeking, when they
were thinking about their mothers, when they were
coming out as a gay man.

The men with whom I worked for three years began
to take on the characteristics not necessarily of a pack,
but of needy children with developmental issues. They
were circling for position in some natural order of
instinct and personalities were beginning to clash.

Many were there to enjoy the resources and develop their own projects, but some were very muddled about who they were and the nature of their own reality.

There was a risk of dependence for the wrong reasons and which, for other teachers, was cancelled out by the fact that they did not interact with individuals for longer than the three weeks of whichever course they were delivering. The boundaries were tighter. Other teachers didn't get to know the personal background of Tony who could not spell, only the specifics of his education. But I had more information about Tony's reality because I had spent more time with him and because he had revealed himself in his writing. I felt for Tony but the feelings were inchoate and had to be constantly processed and managed.

I could have taken the path to desensitisation, detachment and acceptance, as most professionals working in this area have to, but I was fortunate to have a choice. I did not have to contract what the former Inspector of Prisons, Nick Hardwicke, called 'prison horror fatigue'. Having visited most prisons, and been appalled by many, during his five years in tenure, he left the job, saying it was necessary to do so if one was to maintain one's sense of outrage at the state of it all, particularly the Young Offenders Institutions.

While the National Offender Management Service attempted to prescribe every moment of every day with minutely detailed instructions, order and reviews, the human beings on the front line and serving time moved along in a parallel universe where everything was unnatural and occasionally very heightened.

I found myself in the dark once, in a corridor; the lights had gone out for no reason and I was escorting a lifer who had been imprisoned for jumping out at women and sexually assaulting them in dark alleys. I felt a bit nervous. 'It's very dark,' I kept saying, peering through the ink. 'Why aren't the lights on?' His form walked silently beside me as a lugubrious shadow and my heart began to beat. 'Don't worry, Jess,' he replied. 'I feel very safe with you.'

Lightning Source UK Ltd.
Milton Keynes UK
UKOW01f2135310117
293268UK00004B/146/P